S0-BYA-079

the Cloth·paper scissors® BOOK

Techniques and Inspiration for Creating Mixed-Media Art

barbara delaney

INTERWEAVE.
interweave.com

Editor	Elaine Lipson
Art Director	Liz Quan
Designer	Karla Baker
Photography	Larry Stein and Korday Studios
Production	Katherine Jackson

Additional Photography
page 101: Elizabeth St. Hilaire Nelson
page 105: Doug Nelson

© 2011 Interweave Press LLC

All rights reserved.

All of the articles in this collection were previously published in *Cloth Paper Scissors* magazine, ©Interweave. Some have been altered to update information or conform to space limitations.

Interweave Press LLC
201 East Fourth Street
Loveland, CO 80537
interweave.com

Printed in China by C&C Offset.

Library of Congress Cataloging-in-Publication Data

The cloth paper scissors book : techniques and inspiration for creating mixed-media art / [edited by] Barbara Delaney.
    p. cm.
 Includes bibliographical references and index.
 ISBN 978-1-59668-397-6 (pbk.)
 1. Mixed media (Art) 2. Collage. 3. Paperwork. 4. Sewing.
I. Delaney, Barbara, 1954- II. Cloth, paper, scissors.
 TT157.C527 2011
 702.8'1--dc22

                        2011007766

10 9 8 7 6 5 4 3 2 1

Acknowledgments

A heartfelt thank you to all of the contributors whose amazing work is a part of this book, and to everyone who has shared in *Cloth Paper Scissors* over the years. It was an honor and a pleasure to work with each and every one of you.

A special thank you to Patricia (Pokey) and John Bolton for giving me this opportunity, to Kate Binder and Larissa Davis for their help, and to my editor, Elaine Lipson, who made it all come together.

And to my wonderful kids—Alli, Ryan, and Evan—and to Lee. Thank you for being so patient and understanding.

CONTENTS

Introduction: A Note from Barbara   6

1 BEGINNING   8

A Beginner's Guide to Beginning *Jodi Ohl*   10

Extra: Mixed-Media Toolbox   14

Idea to Image *Laura Cater-Woods*   16

Extra: Mixed-Media Glossary   20

My Thread Sketch Journey *Kelli Nina Perkins*   22

2 PRINTMAKING AND SURFACE DESIGN   26

Mixed-Media Watercolor Techniques *Jacqueline Sullivan*   28

Building Upon Layers: Detailed Design Made Easy *Beryl Taylor*   36

Texture and Layers with Acrylic Paint and Stencils *Lisa Kesler* 40

Translucent Transfers *DJ Pettitt*   44

Extra: Paper Alternatives   51

Making Gelatin Monoprints *Jenn Mason*   52

3 JOURNALS AND BOOKMAKING   56

Keeping Creative Sketchbooks *Jane LaFazio*   58

The Meander Book *Susie LaFond*   62

Extra: Easy Book Binding   67

Art Journaling: Pages in Stages *Dawn DeVries Sokol*   68

Travel Journals: Maps as a Starting Point *Jacqueline Newbold*   74

If These Walls Could Talk: Home Journaling *Lynn Whipple*   78

4 COLLAGE AND ASSEMBLAGE 82

Stop! Look! Listen! Recycling Your World Into Art
*The Oiseaux Sisters, Susan Andrews and
Carolyn Fellman* 84

The Mixed Adventures of a Superhero Series
June Pfaff Daley 90

Cupcake Concoctions *Sue Pelletier* 96

Extra: 25 Found Objects + 50 Papers to Collect 99

All Torn Up: An Approach to Collage
Elizabeth St. Hilaire Nelson 100

Character Study: Text as a Collage Element
Lisa Occhipinti 106

5 MIXED-MEDIA STITCHING 110

Paper Collage Quilts *Annette Morgan* 112

Mix and Stitch *Dorit Elisha* 116

Sealed with a Stitch *Viv Sliwka* 1120

Extra: Four Easy Handstitches 123

6 MIXED MEDIA AND BEYOND: 124
ENCAUSTIC, METAL,
AND JEWELRY

The Encaustic Collage
Patricia Baldwin Seggebruch 126

Extra: Make It Stick: A Guide to Adhesives 131

Metal Magic *Beryl Taylor* 132

Metal Heads: Image Transfers on Metal
Janette Schuster 136

Dipped and Delightful: Paper Beads
Kelli Nina Perkins 142

7 GET YOUR ART OUT THERE! 148

Heavens to Etsy! *Cate Coulacos Prato* 150

10 Tips for Selling Your Art During Hard Times
Cate Coulacos Prato 152

Meet the Contributors 156
Resources 158
Index 159

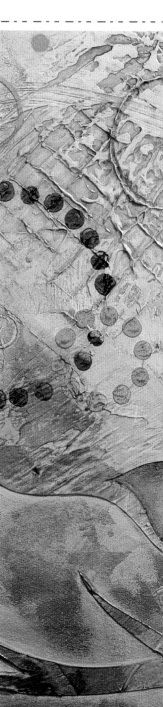

7085
2½x5 in.10c.
Top of umbrella case.

6840
4x4½ in.5c.

6841
4¼ in.5c.

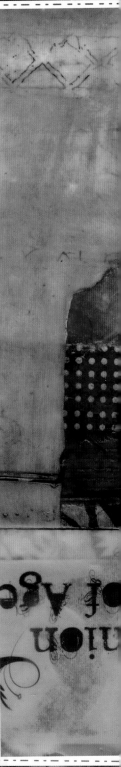

I was very happy and excited to join the *Quilting Arts* team in 2003. I learned a lot about art quilting and all that it entails, and I enjoyed every minute. A short time later, Patricia (Pokey) Bolton had another great idea, and soon *Cloth Paper Scissors* magazine was born. We were all thrilled to welcome this new publication to the family. New artists, new techniques, and new materials excite and inspire us with each issue. I am the assistant editor of *Cloth Paper Scissors*, and it has been a wonderful experience.

When I was asked to do this book, I was delighted. With so many great articles to choose from, the only problem was trying to select the ones to include! Going over past issues was a trip down memory lane; remembering artists, events, and experiences was time well spent and a lot of fun. It was tough to get the articles down to a manageable group, but I did, and I think you'll be pleased with the selection.

The Cloth Paper Scissors Book: Techniques and Inspiration for Creating Mixed-Media Art offers an assortment of articles from past issues of *Cloth Paper Scissors* magazine, along with some extra tips and resources to help you find your niche in mixed media. With everything from collage and bookmaking to encaustic and stitch, *The Cloth Paper Scissors Book* delivers an abundance of inspirations to keep you creating. If you're new to mixed media, you'll find new ideas, direction, and exciting projects to get you going. And if you're a veteran but find yourself sticking with your tried-and-true materials and methods, this book will show you that there is a lot more waiting for you and will help you take the leap to try something different. Soon you, too, will be mixing your media.

CHAPTER 1

BEGINNING

Getting started is often the most difficult part of making art. Sometimes you have a germ of an idea and just can't get going; other times you want to try a new product but need the inspiration. Finding that inspiration, choosing materials and tools, and encountering new terminology and techniques can stop you in your tracks. In this chapter, you'll find a glossary of terms, a short list of materials and tools to get you started, and a longer list for when you're ready to really spread your wings. You'll also find inspiring words and projects from some of our favorite artists.

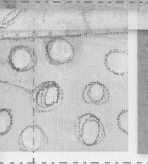

a beginner's guide to
BEGINNING

by **jodi ohl**

Belonging 5¾" × 4" (14.5 × 10 cm)

How has an emerging artist without formal training managed to lead a creative life? I get asked this question all the time. I don't have a magic formula, but I do know that it boils down to making choices. It's about deciding to do something and taking action to make it happen. Seriously. We all have the same twenty-four hours a day. It's what you do with that time that makes the difference.

Make a commitment to do something, anything, every day to make your creative life a real part of your daily routine. And have a plan so you know where to direct your creative commitments as you work toward reaching your artistic goals.

Decide what you want your creative world to look like. Remember, you can't move forward if you don't at least start to take action.

Coming Home 12" × 6" (30.5 x 15 cm)

HOW TO GET STARTED

A journal is a great way to get all of your creative ideas and artistic goals in one place. Here are some prompts:

Who are you? Write a ten-second introduction of yourself as an artist. You need to have an "elevator" story prepared for everyone you meet in order to be able to engage a potential client (or at the very least someone who is interested in your art) in a way that clearly describes what it is that you do and why they should be interested in your work. Practice and refine your introduction so that you can say it naturally.

What do you want to do? Instead of thinking about where you want to be in five years, think about the top three things you want to accomplish in the next twelve months. Do you want to be published? Perhaps you want to do an outdoor show this year or submit your work to a local gallery. Maybe one of your goals is to open an Etsy shop or another online sales venue.

Whatever your top three artistic goals are, write them down and be as descriptive as possible. You also need to insert a deadline so you can hold yourself accountable. For example, "I want to be published three times in a national art magazine this year. In order to do so, I will submit my work every other month to maximize the chance of having my work accepted."

How are you going to do this? Evaluate your schedule—what time of day are you most creative? If you only

TIPS *to get you started*

→ **Make To-Do Lists** I'm a list maker. I start with what I want to do over the course of a year and then break it down into smaller time slots. I list the things I want to do each month and determine my top projects. I re-evaluate my progress each week and make adjustments.

→ **Create a Planner** I've started using a planner to organize my creative goals. This way I can actually look at the time frame that I commit to a project. I have learned to build in some cushion, because there are always things that come up to throw your plan off track. Plan for the unexpected, and it won't be an issue.

→ **Form a Support Group** Enlist some of your creative friends to get together monthly (or more often). Have play dates or perhaps a more formal structure to talk about business tips, technique questions, or even to critique each other's work. When others are holding you accountable, it inspires you to get serious.

→ **Start a Blog** A blog is a perfect platform to track your progress as an artist and be cheered along the way by supporters from all over the world. There is something about putting yourself out there and meeting people who not only understand your passion but encourage you to continually do more that gets you going.

→ **Work in Themes and Collections** Think about working in themes and collections. While experimenting is wonderful and needed in every aspect of a creative life, at some point you have to narrow your focus and refine your skills, play out your themes, and eventually create a body of work that is cohesive. Think about what you want to focus on and start planning.

→ **Take Pictures** When going through a dry spell, don't despair. Go for a walk with your camera and take some unusual shots. Look for color and texture inspiration wherever you travel. You can use these recorded images in numerous ways (collage, paintings, fabric transfers, digital collage, etc.), and they provide a pool of ideas to pull from when you need them.

→ **Capture Your Ideas** If you aren't a journal writer, think about getting a sketchbook to document interesting ideas, corral your lists, doodle, and to have a single place to reference for future inspiration. Your commitment to do something every day to make your artistic life more real includes journal writing and sketching! Some days it can be simple, it's just the point of doing something every day.

have a short period of time each day to create, start by deciding when it is that you are at your best, then carve out that time to be creative and stick to it. If you are a morning person but you work a day job and need to get the kids off to school every day, too, maybe it's going to mean you have to get up an hour or two earlier each day to make that happen. Come up with a creative schedule and put art time into your calendar just as you would a dentist or hair appointment.

How do you start?
Now that you've made up your mind to be productive and are committed to doing something every day, go back to your top three goals and start an idea file so you can work toward achieving your goals in an organized fashion. For example, if one of your goals this year is to create a body of work to present to a regional gallery, create a file to stash ideas for your theme. Perhaps include photographic examples that inspire you. Do whatever it takes to start working on your projects and goals. I've seen too many people blocked by the fear of starting a project and making excuses as to why they can't accomplish something instead of simply starting somewhere and producing work.

How are you going to financially afford to live the creative life?
Start small and plan big. You may not be able to buy the best materials or all the equipment you want right away, but you can open a savings account dedicated solely to your

artistic endeavors and start saving for the day when you can accumulate the things you want. I decided long ago to separate my art money from my regular household funds, and it has really helped me to rein in my expenditures.

Design a budget that includes supplies, professional dues, marketing efforts, show fees, travel expenses, salary, savings and investments, and of course taxes, along with any other items that may be unique to your art or your situation. Even if you only have a vague idea of how much everything costs, if you start with a budget and a rough idea of how much it is that you are willing to spend/invest, you may be more inspired to stick to it and actually produce enough work to pay for it all.

Once you have these things in place, it's up to you to put the plan to work. Remember, it's all about choices. Don't be too hard on yourself if you feel like you aren't keeping up with someone else. It's not about them; it's about you and your dreams. Conversely, don't be too easy on yourself either. Simply take action and follow your dreams. Start now—not tomorrow, not the next day, not when things settle down in your world. I only manage doing it all by simply doing. Even then, it's not necessarily doing it all, but it will always be more than if you opt to do nothing. ✳

EXTRA

mixed-media TOOLBOX

Mixed-media art calls for a variety of supplies. As you experiment and try new items and techniques, you'll add new products and tools to your arsenal. Remember to replenish supplies as you use them. There is nothing more frustrating than being in the middle of a project and running out of something. Depending on your area of interest, the supplies you stock will vary, but this very basic list will get you started. If you're unfamiliar with any of these items, refer to the glossary on page 20.

basic mixed-media materials

- ☐ **acrylic paints**
- ☐ **bone folder**
- ☐ **craft knife, self-healing cutting mat, and ruler**
- ☐ **craft/tacky glue**
- ☐ **fabric scraps**
- ☐ **found objects and papers**
- ☐ **glue sticks**
- ☐ **journal and sketchbook**
- ☐ **paintbrushes** in various sizes and shapes
- ☐ **paper and paper scraps** in a variety of types, weights, and textures
- ☐ **scissors** for fabric and paper and a small sharp pair for details
- ☐ **soft gel medium**
- ☐ **substrates**, such as canvas board, mat board, and wood
- ☐ **writing tools** including pencils, pens, and markers.

As you build your stash, add some or all of the items below, depending on where your muse takes you.

- [ ] **adhesives** such as repositionable glue, PVA, Glue Dots, Pop Dots, E-6000, Liquid Nails, Sobo, spray fixative, gel medium

- [ ] **awl**

- [ ] **cosmetic foam wedges and cotton swabs**

- [ ] **Dremel rotary tool:** A power tool that accepts multiple bits for various activities such as drilling, sanding, polishing, grinding, cutting, and engraving.

- [ ] **fibers** such as string, twine, ribbon, yarn, embroidery floss, thread

- [ ] **found objects**

- [ ] **fusible web** such as WonderUnder, Steam-A-Seam, or Mistyfuse

- [ ] **gesso**

- [ ] **heat gun**

- [ ] **India ink and walnut ink**

- [ ] **iron and ironing pad**

- [ ] **oil sticks**

- [ ] **pens/markers** such as Micron, Pitt, Sharpie, bleach, gel, etc.

- [ ] **pinking shears, decorative scissors, or paper punches**

- [ ] **pliers** needle-nose, flat-nose

- [ ] **rubbing plates**

- [ ] **sewing machine and sewing supplies**

- [ ] **stamps and stamp pads**

- [ ] **stencils**

- [ ] **tapes** such as clear, paper tape, masking, painter's, double-sided, florist, drywall, duct, decorative

- [ ] **watercolor paints**

- [ ] **water-soluble stabilizer:** This fine polyvinyl fabric feels like very thin plastic; when doubled in an embroidery hoop and stitched on, it's ideal for creating lacy patterns. The stabilizer disappears with immersion in hot water, leaving just the embroidery.

IDEA *to* IMAGE

by **laura cater-woods**

Maze Book, a meditation on bark, by Cornelia Jutta Forster

After what has seemed like months away from your artwork you finally have time to work in the studio—and your brain seems blank. You have no clue what you will do with all this time and freedom. Several hours later you realize that all you have done is check your email, play solitaire, move one pile of raw materials from point A to point B, and answer the telephone, only to chat with fund-raisers.

Or perhaps your brain is swimming with ideas, and you can't wait to get to work. But once you are in the studio you cannot focus, cannot find a place to start.

What is going on here? Are you blocked? Succumbing to doubt and thinking you're not really an artist?

Actually, it is not unusual for creative people to be intimidated by the blank space, the empty canvas, the pressure of generating something from nothing. Regardless of our experience level, we are all occasionally overwhelmed by the concept of taking the tools and materials we love to use, combining them with our current skill level, and creating an image uniquely our own. Where do we start?

CREATING RITUALS

Whether it is a bedroom closet or space in a separate building, consider your art space or studio sacred. It doesn't matter where or how large and well-appointed your studio is, as long as you approach the work with the right attitude. What is essential is that you dedicate a space just for your creative work and celebrate your available time. One artist I know refers to this as "the studio between the ears."

Always approach that space and time as special. Create a small ritual that tells your creative brain that it's time to get to work. Some artists do this with repetitive tasks such as sharpening pencils or laying out paint on a palette just so. Some put on a favorite piece of music, some meditate. Repeating these rituals

when you have creative time available will alert your brain that it is time to stop thinking about the mundane or pressing tasks of daily life and let those creative juices flow.

STARTING TO WORK

Congratulations! You have now taken the biggest, most important step in your creative day. You are in your workspace; you have carved out time. Now what?

If you were in a studio workshop, a facilitator could brainstorm with you or give you an assignment. But here you are, on your own. Where will the ideas come from and where should you start?

My suggestion is the same as it would be if you were in my class. Pay attention to what draws you in or fascinates you in the world outside your imagination. Tropical fish? Sunrises? The daily changes in your garden?

Take notice of what attracts you. It could be:

→ forms repeating themselves in your doodles;

→ subjects that you are continually drawn to in your photographs;

→ previous artwork you have completed (perhaps consider doing a series);

→ particular geometric shapes, colors, textures, or architectural motifs that intrigue you.

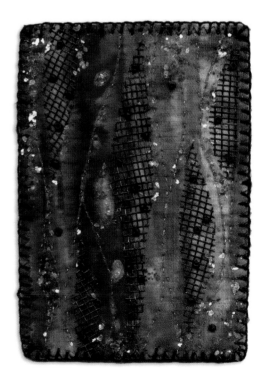

Maybe this approach seems too simple. Consider this: Miro began with tree branches; Monet planted gardens so he could explore changing qualities of light and their impact on color; O'Keeffe is known for her oversized flower studies. These artists began with simple objects that fascinated them. It is the repeated expressions of this imagery that we find compelling and that lead to the big ideas.

Artist Corni Forster began with the idea of trees and narrowed it to bark. In my work, I'm fascinated by a particular spiraling shape that I find everywhere. Sometimes it seems I could easily spend all my time exploring this one idea and not find the end of it.

KEEPING A NOTEBOOK

Take just one form, one shape, one line or color. Get your sketchbook or visual journal and make some notes to yourself focusing on one element you have identified. What colors, textures, sounds, and smells do you associate with the motif? Make notes in words and doodles, paste in scraps of color or text or perhaps collaged elements. These saved ideas become raw material for later use.

Next, make a preliminary sketch or two. Diagram it out—don't try to design the whole piece, just "think out loud" visually. Too much planning at the beginning can result in a finished piece that's stale. Let the creative juices flow.

Now that you have selected an element and thought about arrangement, it's time to start your

Cornelia (Corni) Jutta Forster (whose work *Maze Book, a meditation on bark* illustrates this article) draws much of her inspiration from the natural world.

Her mixed-media work shows a fascination with process and with texture, and it often has a meditative quality. In class, she admitted to being in a high-stress period in her life; she did not have enough time to work and felt stuck—unable to make art at all. I suggested she confine her work to a very small format, the size of a playing card, and to limit herself to one aspect of one part of nature that she was interested in. She decided on tree bark, and in two days, working only with what was at hand, she made twelve small pieces, generated the idea of putting them into book format, and came through her block. It took an idea that seemed manageable to allow Corni to say yes to her work.

journey. Collect your tools and materials, keeping in mind the sensory elements you identified to support the motif. Most artists go into automatic pilot at this stage. Your hands and eyes know what they are doing. Trust them. Trust yourself.

You may also have trouble getting started if your idea is too big. Sometimes you need to break an idea down into its component parts. Ask yourself: What is the most important thing to me about this idea? How does it feel? What words, aromas, and textures do I associate with this element? What colors do I see?

Find one aspect of your idea that you feel you have a handle on and let the image build from there.

GETTING IT DOWN

As you begin to assemble the image you will find yourself in different places. There are moments of deliberation, decisions to be made. Often answers depend on the materials you work with. For example, if you are a painter, there are rules that are based on the physical properties of your medium. The same goes for working with transparencies and glazes. Sometimes an artist's methods determine how an image develops. There are people who always build their images from the center out and others who start at the foreground.

Whatever your first step is, subsequent steps are taken in conversation with the work. This is one reason I do not recommend too much advance planning. Once a color or texture is placed, the adjacent area

must work in relationship to that first choice. Will it contrast in temperature, degree of intensity, texture, or size and scale, or will it be an area that blends? You may not know this ahead of time. Trust your eyes and your intuitive knowledge to guide you. Let the creative you out to play.

Art, like any other worthwhile activity is a matter of discipline, learned skills, and having the correct tools. With regular positive habits we can improve our odds of feeling good about ourselves as artists. Learning to set aside space and time, to respect them both, and to take that important walk into our creative time with clarity, allows us to create and celebrate the artist within. ✳

mixed-media GLOSSARY

This glossary is a brief introduction to terms and products that appear frequently throughout this book. See the resource list on page 158 for suggestions on where to purchase these and other mixed-media supplies.

Angelina fibers: Shiny plastic fibers that create a shimmery fabric that can be cut, stitched, and glued when fused with heat.

Artist Trading Card (ATC): A 2½" x 3½" (6.5 x 9 cm) piece of art backed with felt or a firmer backing such as cardboard. Artists often use them for business cards or trade them for fun.

Bone folder: A tool for marking, scoring, or creasing paper or fabric, especially wherever a sharp crease is needed.

Brayer: A hand roller used in printmaking techniques to spread ink or to offset an image from a plate to paper. Brayers are made from a variety of materials, including rubber, sponge, and acrylic.

Collage: Artwork made from items that are adhered to a surface, such as a piece of paper, canvas, or board, and the technique of making such an artwork. Materials may include papers, foil, metal, plastic, fabric, wire, photographs, paintings, and found objects.

Collography: A printing process using a cut image or a collection of objects glued to a firm surface to create a printing plate. Use anything that creates texture: toothpicks, cord, corks, plastic wrap, etc.

Dry brush: A painting technique where a little bit of paint is put on a dry brush to produce a broken, scratchy effect.

Encaustic: A method of painting that uses pigments melted with wax that are fixed or fused to the painting surface with heat.

Fabric paper: Paper created by layering a variety of papers onto lightweight fabric with a glue wash.

Felt: A nonwoven fabric, often wool, made by pressing fibers together. Felt can be extremely soft or firm enough to be used as a construction material and comes in a variety of colors, shapes, and sizes.

Fixative: A spray acrylic that, when applied to artwork, keeps the medium (paint, ink, pastel, etc.) from smudging.

Fluid acrylic paint: A type of acrylic paint that is fluid relative to heavy-body acrylic paint, with the same intensity of color.

Focal point: The element or object in a painting or a piece of art that draws the viewer's eye to it, or the main subject in a piece of art.

Free-motion stitching: Machine stitching on a fabric or paper surface in any direction, creating geometric, flowing, or random patterns. Sewing machines must be specially equipped for this function or must have the capacity to lower the feed dog (the "teeth" that normally keep the fabric moving through the machine in a straight line).

Fusible web: Very thin sheets of webbed adhesive that can fuse fabrics and other fibers together when activated by heat. Fusible web comes in cut sheets or on a roll and is sometimes housed between two layers of release paper.

Gel medium: An acrylic polymer medium that can accept color media and other additives, such as glitter or fine beads, to create texture when applied to a surface.

Gel pens: Gel-inked ballpoint pens that come in a variety of sizes and colors. The distinguishing characteristic is the gel ink, which is made of pigments suspended in a water-based gel.

Gesso: A thick chalky mixture that can be painted onto paper or fabric to provide a rough-textured base surface.

Hake brush: A soft brush with a long flat handle, used in Oriental painting. Hake brushes are effective for laying in washes (large fluid areas) of water-based paint.

Heat gun: This tool blows hot air in a focused direction in order to melt, heat set, or burn fibers, powders, and other materials.

Heat-set: Using heat (from an iron, heat gun, or clothes dryer) to make dyes, transfers, paints, or inks that have been applied to fabric permanent.

Matte medium: Acrylic polymer medium that can be used to extend paints, increase translucency, and decrease gloss.

Mod Podge: An acid-free brand of glue that is useful as a glue or final layer for collage and decoupage. It is available in gloss, satin, and matte finishes.

Molding paste: A water-based acrylic polymer emulsion that dries to an opaque, semigloss finish that, once dry, will accept acrylic paint and other media.

Mulberry paper: A handmade paper with a lot of texture and edges that feather easily when wet. It's available in a wide range of colors in smooth and textured styles.

Needle felting: Fusing a layer of fiber onto a base fiber or felted fabric. Needle felting can be done by hand with a needle felting brush or piece of foam and felting needle(s), or with a needle-felting machine. In both cases, the fabrics/fibers are layered one on top of the other, and the needle punctures the layers continuously and quickly until they are fused together.

Photo transfer: Photographic images transferred onto fabric using photo transfer paper. First, the photograph is printed onto the paper, which is then ironed onto the fabric, transferring the image.

Repositionable adhesive: A tacky film that allows you to stick fabric or paper in one place and then move it without harming the substrate, usually paper, underneath. It comes in tape, dots, sprays, etc.

Screen printing: Also referred to as serigraphy and silk screening, this is a printing technique that uses a woven mesh screen to print onto fabric. A stencil is attached to the screen, and only the areas left exposed allow the ink to transfer through as a roller or squeegee is used to apply the ink across the surface of the screen and onto the fabric underneath.

Sobo glue: A brand of general-purpose white glue that dries fast and clear.

Stippling: A faux painting technique that gives new surfaces an elegant, aged look made by repeatedly tapping on a surface with paint or ink and a stiff brush. While most methods of faux painting hide imperfections, stippling actually highlights them. It is best done on surfaces in excellent condition.

Transfer: Applying ink-jet or toner copy images to fabric using different media, such as water, polymers, and other media.

Underpainting: The initial or lowest layers of paint put down in a painting before the detail of the painting is put down. Some artists use underpainting to establish tonal values in a painting, effectively painting a monochrome version of the final painting to get all the tones right before adding color. Others use underpainting to establish areas of color as a first step in building up colors.

Walnut ink: Made from walnuts, this very dark ink can be used to "age" papers and other materials and to tone down bright colors.

Water-soluble fabric: Fabric that disappears in cold or hot water (depending on the brand and its use) after it has been stitched on, leaving only the stitching.

Water-soluble stabilizer: A fine polyvinyl fabric that feels like very thin plastic; when doubled in an embroidery hoop and stitched on, it's ideal for creating lacy patterns. The stabilizer disappears with immersion in hot water, leaving just the embroidery.

my THREAD SKETCH *journey*

by **kelli nina perkins**

~ sketches ~

The dilemma of finding new inspiration plagues every artist now and then, myself included. On sunny days, creative lightning strikes with wild abandon, and I scurry to keep up with the ideas buzzing in my brain. On other days, I scour the landscape without finding a single spark of creative fire, and that's when artistic recycling often comes to my rescue. Creative recyclers dig in the fertile soil of their completed projects to find small seeds they can transplant. By layering skills and techniques you've been playing with all along, you can achieve a richer, deeper expression of personal art.

Keeping a mixed-media idea journal can encourage your seeds of inspiration to germinate and grow. In my "What If" journal, I take techniques from successful projects and visualize them across other media. What if I used a different material or tried a different shape? No idea is too silly to be explored. This "doodlestorming" serves as a constant source of

inspiration and often provides the fertilizer for nurturing new projects.

When a recent month-long Everyday Art project proved challenging, I pulled out my journal and looked for ways to recycle some ingredients. I chose a dozen fabulous new methods to pursue, but a few days later I was already struggling. I decided to simplify and concentrate on pen-

and-ink drawings. I recalled studying Matisse's works at the Institute of Art in Detroit. There I would glory in the happy color of his work. His sketches looked hasty and unrefined, but they captured the very essence of his subject. Channeling my favorite modern master, I put pen to paper and abandoned notions of perfectly drawn compositions.

A few drawings later, I was still disappointed. Perplexed, I wandered through my mixed-media journal and found that I'd doodled about outlining various items in thread, including paintings on paper! I hadn't actually done it, I'd only visualized it in my journal, but this was the seed I needed. Once I added thread sketching to these simple compositions, they sang to me. I had discovered a quick technique that transformed my rudimentary brushstrokes into finished works of art: thread sketching.

When applied to artist trading cards, greeting cards, framed paintings, journals, and altered books, thread adds a surprising textural dimension. Because sketching with thread is nearly as versatile as sketching with pen, you can make your sketch any size you'd like. You are limited only by the amount of paper you can negotiate within the throat of your sewing machine. Even then, you can create multiple smaller sketches and assemble them into a larger piece. Choose a sheet of nice, heavy watercolor paper and a good waterproof pen for fine-line drawing.

- - - - - - - - - - - - - - - - - - - -

tip: Since navigating small pieces of paper around the sewing machine is difficult, you may want to work on larger paper and cut out artist trading cards or smaller pieces after you have stitched them.

materials

- ☐ Watercolor paper (90 or 140 lb)
- ☐ Pencil
- ☐ Eraser
- ☐ Pigma Micron pen or technical pen
- ☐ Book pages for collage
- ☐ Glue stick
- ☐ Watercolor paints
- ☐ Paintbrushes
- ☐ Sewing machine
- ☐ Black thread

early morning greeting

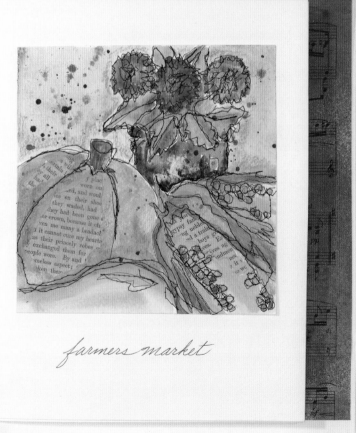

farmers market

If you are a veteran sketcher, create a simple pen sketch of your favorite subject; for the rest of us, here is a quick and dirty technique for getting started.

1 Print out a photo you've taken of something relatively simple, like a vase of flowers or a garden scene.

2 With permanent marker, outline the major elements. This is what you'll re-create on your paper. Don't worry about the small details; just capture the essence of the image by focusing on the important components and basic shapes.

3 Mentally divide up your watercolor paper and loosely sketch the images with pen. Sometimes it's helpful to use a pencil first for placement. If I'm drawing a large pumpkin and a bunch of smaller ones, I'll create pencil circles where I want my elements to appear. Be sure to erase any extra pencil markings before moving to the next step.

tip: Determine what's in the foreground and what's in the background and draw the closer objects first.

4 Your lines do not have to be perfect, but try to draw in a single line rather than feathered short strokes. You'll be stitching over this line with your sewing machine, and at that time you can add a more sketched look. Close up all of your shapes so that you have areas to fill with watercolor. Keep in mind that this kind of sketching is more about representative shapes than subtleties.

5 Now tear some pages out of an old book. I love to use strange things like gambling texts or scientific literature, but it's also fun to weave poetry throughout your collage. Choose something to complement your drawing and tear shapes that echo the lines in your drawing. Use a glue stick to attach them to some of the open areas, sprinkling them around in a way that pleases you. Use them to illustrate shadow or highlights or just to fill big areas.

tip: Ripping produces a more organic look that allows the text to fade into the background after it's painted.

6 Fill a jar with water and a variety of paintbrushes. Using whatever watercolors you have on hand, begin filling in the areas with paint, covering the collaged text. For a more ethereal look, wet the paper first. The watercolors will bleed and blend and ignore your drawn lines, but you can sop up any parts you don't like with a clean brush. Painting on dry paper is a little easier, but try both methods to see which you prefer.

tip: You can fill an entire space with one go of the paintbrush, but to add more visual interest, pick up a little more color on your brush and go over the space again, blending so that some areas are more saturated. This is really

a very easy process, so don't worry about making it look perfect; just get the color down and fill your spaces.

7 To add a little excitement, take a brush, get it wet, then dip it in one of the colors you've already used and shake it over the painting with a snap of your wrist to create flecks of color. Do this while some areas of the paper are still wet, and the flecks will alter the way the watercolor dries by creating resists and textured splotches. Aim for splashing similar colors together. This will create an illusion of movement and pattern. If you have a yellow background, splash various shades of ocher and yellow to create depth. If you are enhancing a pink flower, use flecks of dark pink, red, and even white to create contrasts and make it look like the flower is exploding beyond the confines of your pen line. When the paint is dry, you can move on to stitching.

stitching

1 Your sketch should give the impression of being quickly or loosely drawn, whether it actually happened that way or not. I've chosen to use black thread to imitate India ink, but once you've practiced you might want to try other colors for contrast. Set up your sewing machine for free-motion quilting. A free-motion (or darning) foot, available for most machines, is helpful so that the sketch can be moved smoothly

in any direction while stitching. Retract the feed dog or cover it with an optional plate so that its teeth are not in the way. Use a denim needle for sewing through heavy paper and do some test stitching on a piece of scrap watercolor paper of the same weight you plan to use before you begin. You may find that you have to adjust the thread tension.

tip: Experimenting on scrap paper is important, since stitched paper cannot really be unstitched and each machine is different. Once the holes are poked, they are permanent, even if you do remove the stitching. Work out as many issues as possible before you start stitching on your painting.

2 Select a straight stitch, place your sketch under the needle, and pick an entry point anywhere on your pen line. I'd suggest starting at one end or the other, as the less you have to stop and cut the thread, the better. Place your palms firmly on either side of your sketch and begin following your drawn line with the needle by moving the paper with gentle pressure. It may help to set your stitch speed to a slower setting at first. However, I find that I like to work fast, because it's more truly sketched that way.

3 Follow the lines of your sketch without cutting the thread by re-stitching over lines two or three times (if necessary) to get to other areas of the painting, as if you were making a drawing without

picking the pen up from the paper. It's scary to do this because it may feel as if you've made a mistake, but imperfection adds to the beauty of these pieces.

tip: There may be interior areas to be stitched that are isolated from the other lines. It's okay to cut the thread and start over in another area. Just try to do this as little as possible.

When you've covered each pen line once, or maybe more, remove your finished thread sketch from the machine and admire your handiwork. Your painting is ready to be incorporated into other projects or framed. For my sketchbook, I stitched the title text on a separate piece of watercolor paper and glued all of the thread sketches to larger pages bound with a pamphlet stitch. ✳

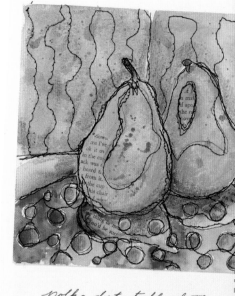

polka dot tablecloth and pears

CHAPTER **2**

PRINTMAKING AND
surface design

There seems to be no limit to the media and techniques that artists are discovering and using to make art today: household items are used to create wonderful backgrounds and prints, everyday objects add texture and dimension, and things that would have ended up in the trash a few years ago turn into tools for stamping and mark making. In this chapter, mixed-media artists present their art and techniques in ways that will have you adding to your stash and to your artistic repertoire.

mixed-media
WATERCOLOR *techniques*

by jacqueline sullivan

When we think of watercolor painting, images of flower bouquets or serene landscapes often come to mind. However, one does not need to know how to paint a scene or a still life (or want to) in order to enjoy the lush beauty and benefits of watercolor paints. A few years ago, I began experimenting by adding other media to my watercolor paints and was amazed with the resulting papers. I use transparent watercolor techniques with mixed media to create colorful, textured backgrounds for my calligraphic works, collage, mixed media, and handmade books.

materials

- [ ] Several plastic water bottles with squirt-top caps
- [ ] Transparent watercolors
- [ ] Watercolor paper
- [ ] A shallow tray (such as an edged cookie sheet)
- [ ] Spray bottle
- [ ] Small palette
- [ ] Distilled water
- [ ] 2 large containers for water
- [ ] An inexpensive flat 1" (2.5 cm) brush
- [ ] Masonite board (optional)

USING TRANSPARENT WATERCOLORS

The trick to mixing transparent watercolors is to mix the color with the water before it is applied to the paper. After you premix the colors, use the plastic water bottle to pour them on the paper, rather than using the traditional palette and brush. By minimizing direct contact with the paper surface, you will achieve transparent color with glazing. Glazing is a technique of layering transparent colors over one another, allowing the colors underneath to shine through the top color.

colors and paints

It is best to stay within a limited palette. A palette of primary colors (red, yellow, and blue) plus some earth colors will help build shadows and tonal qualities. While you are learning, it is a good idea to have no more than three colors on your paper; they will blend and form other colors. Make your fourth color a neutral. I use Payne's gray as a neutral color. It blends with all colors and quiets down some of the more brilliant colors. Some brands of

burnt umber also work well as a neutralizing color.

One group of premixed colors that I use is alizarin crimson, phthalo blue, hansa yellow, quinacridone gold, sap green, burnt sienna, and Payne's gray. I sometimes add burnt umber, quinacridone violet, and yellow ocher. In addition to having these premixed colors in bottles, a small palette with the same colors on it can be used to enhance areas of color while the paper is wet.

My preferred brands of watercolor paints are American Journey or Daniel Smith. Less expensive brands of paint can be grainy and pale, but both of these brands offer a wide range of colors of fairly good quality. Pigments from different manufacturers are usually compatible. For these techniques, you just need to be sure that you are using transparent watercolors. However, be aware that colors with the same name will vary from one manufacturer to another, and some experimentation may be necessary to find a palette that works for you.

PAINTING
mixing the paint

To mix the paint, put a small amount of water in the bottom of a bottle. Add about ½ tsp (2.5 ml) of paint to the water and shake to mix. Add another 4 oz (119 ml) of water to the bottle and shake again, thoroughly dissolving all of the pigment. The strength of pigment varies greatly from one manufacturer to another. These proportions may be changed depending on the depth of color you are looking for.

After you have your paints mixed and have selected your paper, it is time to prepare your work area. Be sure to have all of the listed materials on hand. You may want to have a few other colors for adding details to your paintings. Fill the spray bottle with clear water. The shallow tray is necessary for catching drips and excess paint. One of the large containers is for clean water to wet your paper, and the second is for rinsing brushes. The flat brush is for pushing the paint a bit. You may also want a round brush for some minimal detailing.

1   With your paper flat, use the spray bottle to wet the paper in areas where you want paint colors to flow and mix. It should be damp (wet but no puddles). After you wet the paper, brush the water out evenly into the area that you are going to paint. If you want more control, use a 2" (5 cm) wash brush to spread the water onto the paper.

2   Shake your first bottle of color to mix it and then pour on some paint. Tilt and rotate your board to get the color moving, letting the excess drip into your shallow pan.

3   Before adding another color, let the first color find its place on the paper and rest a bit, or you will just keep washing the first color off with the next.

4   When your first paint has found its place and is not collecting in puddles, add a second color. Choose analogous colors (colors that are next to each other on the color wheel) such as yellow to green to blue or alizarin to violet to blue. If you cross over the color wheel and use complementary colors, you will get a muddy brown color when the colors run together.

PAPER

It is important to go with a name brand of paper because inexpensive watercolor paper will only frustrate you. Winsor & Newton, Arches, Fabriano, and Lanaquarelle are all good brands of watercolor paper. Watercolor paper usually comes in 90, 140, and 300 lb (190, 300, 638 gsm) weights. The 90 lb (190 gsm) paper is the lightest and is good for book pages and for making decorative papers to cover board for book covers. It does, however, have to be stretched and taped to a board for working because it buckles when wet. Suitable for anything that calls for cardstock, 140 lb (300 gsm) paper is heavy enough for stand-alone covers of books, and it will hold up to scraping, spraying, and pouring of wet media. Heavy and strong, 300 lb (638 gsm) paper is great for a base for collage work.

There are three main types of watercolor paper to choose from: rough, hot press, and cold press.

Rough is suited for dry brush and textural techniques.

Hot-press is pressed with heat in the manufacturing process to give it a very smooth surface. But because there are no hills and valleys on hot-press paper, it is easy for the pigment to just slide off when working very wet.

Cold-press has some hills and valleys, but not as many nor are they as deep as with rough paper. Cold-press papers take wet-in-wet smoothly, allowing the pigment to blend softly and freely.

COLORS

Transparent watercolors can be classified in three categories: earth colors, mineral colors, and dye (or carbon) colors.

Earth colors include umbers, ochers, and oxides and are made from ground earth, such as mineral-rich soils or clay. These colors tend to be heavy, grainy, and not as saturated as other colors. Some special effects, particularly the salt and alcohol techniques, usually do not work with the earth colors.

Mineral colors are inorganic. This classification includes all cadmiums, ultramarines, and cobalt blues. These colors are brilliant and somewhat opaque. Special effects work on these colors but not as dramatically as on the carbon colors.

Carbon or dye colors are organic and staining. They include alizarin crimson, phthalo blue, phthalo green, and viridian colors. These colors are very strong and actually stain the paper. Some can be fugitive, that is, they fade with time. But special effects used on these colors are very dramatic.

Watercolor paintings cut up, woven, and layered into a new piece of art.

This method will give you a beautiful flowing watercolor wash. It makes a great background or abstract on its own, or you can go further and use some additional techniques to give it more texture and interest.

→ The best types of containers to use are plastic water bottles with sport tops (tops that pull to open and squirt). These bottles give you the ability to control the direction of the pigment and to pour on the color. Select bottles with relatively flat bottoms, rather than bottles with conical shapes on the inside bottom. Any creases and/or recessed shapes in the bottom of the bottle tend to trap the pigment.

→ Use distilled water for mixing. This keeps the paint from forming mold; premixed paints are then usable from one painting session to the next.

→ If you are working larger than 11" × 15" (28 x 38 cm), you will want to stretch your watercolor paper onto a board. I use a piece of ¼" (6 mm) finished Masonite for this. As some Masonite will bleed and stain when wet, seal the board first with an acrylic medium and allow to dry. Then tape your paper down solidly with masking tape on all four edges, pulling it tight. This way you can tip and turn the board and paper to get the paint to flow where you want it.

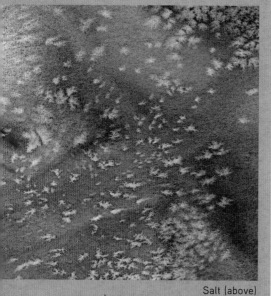

Salt (above)

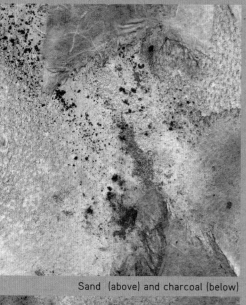

Sand (above) and charcoal (below)

MORE TECHNIQUES TO EXPLORE

salt

Adding salt to the painting makes starlike white shapes in the paint as the salt pushes away the paint colors, creating light spots in the wash. You can use different types of salt (table salt, kosher salt, etc.) to get different-size stars. Salt works better on dye or carbon colors; it has very little effect on the earth colors, and the effect is less dramatic on the mineral colors.

Sprinkle the salt on the paper when you see the wash just begin to lose its shine. You only need a few grains. Don't overdo it or your painting will look like it has the measles. The different types of papers will also change the look of the salt effect. If you tilt your paper so that wet pigment flows through the salt, you will get white streaks that resemble miniature comets in your colored wash.

sand

Sand has the opposite effect of salt in that it makes a dark texture in the wash. Try different textures of sand for different looks; you will be amazed at the number of textures there are in various sands. In my studio, there are containers marked East Coast sand, West Coast sand, play sand, and even aquarium gravel.

For an even more interesting effect, mix the sand and salt together. Stretch your imagination further and see what tiny glass beads or sawdust will do. And how many textures of sawdust are there? This is the fun of experimentation!

charcoal

For a dark, moody look in your watercolor wash, try some powdered charcoal, which is available in most art supply stores. Powdered pastels can also be used in this manner to lighten up areas that have gotten too dark or muddy in the original wash. Pastels give the wash a powdery, airbrushed look.

1   Apply the powdered charcoal to your paper and then spray it with water from your spray bottle to spread it.

2   Let this dry for a few minutes and then do your wash over the top of the charcoal. All of your colors will mix with the charcoal and darken, making your painting very moody. The tonal quality of the original charcoal wash will show through the subsequent colors.

3   When completely dried, lightly spray the matte fixative over entire piece.

metallics

Powdered metallics add drama to the charcoal and pastel techniques. I like to use Daniel Smith metallic watercolors because they already have gum arabic in them, which helps powdered pigments adhere to the wash. Other metallics can be used as well, including Pearl-Ex.

1. Shake the powdered pigment lightly onto a wet wash. Some will dissolve and some will stay in powder form. If you put them over the dark charcoal powder or over a brilliant pastel color, the effect is quite dramatic and beautiful. Excess metallic powder can be brushed off once the painting has dried.

2. For added drama, alcohol can be used on the metallic powders and the crater shapes created by the alcohol will be outlined in gold, silver, or copper.

3. When completely dried, lightly spray the fixative over entire piece.

materials

- ☐ Salt (any type)
- ☐ Sand
- ☐ Denatured alcohol
- ☐ Charcoal (powder or stick)
- ☐ Powdered metallics
- ☐ Rit dye
- ☐ Powdered pigments
- ☐ Dust mask
- ☐ Spray matte fixative
- ☐ Golden Absorbent Ground
- ☐ Plastic wrap, waxed paper, or aluminum foil
- ☐ Oriental papers, tissue paper
- ☐ Fluid matte medium

alcohol

Another technique to add to your bag of tricks is to use alcohol. Alcohol also pushes away the pigment and leaves the white of the paper to show through. Try dropping the alcohol onto a glaze of two colors. The first color should be dry and the second one damp. It will show through the next color layer when the alcohol is dropped onto the damp second color. There are different types of alcohol and each one gives a slightly different effect. For the most dramatic effect, it is best to use denatured alcohol. Available at most hardware stores, it is often labeled as shellac thinner.

Alcohol can be applied in a few different ways. You can mist it on from a spray bottle, which gives an effect similar to the salt technique but without the starlike quality. Again, timing is important. You need to work on the wash after it starts to dry but while it is still shiny and damp. If you put the alcohol on while the paint is too wet, it will be diluted by the wash water and have no effect. If you put it on when the paint is too dry, it can't move the pigment to form a mark. Another option is to apply the alcohol using an eyedropper or pipette. This gives you a crater effect. Several drops in one area form an interesting, dramatic texture.

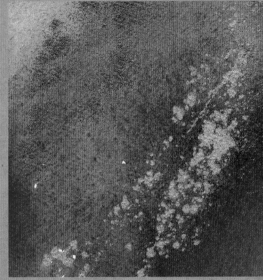

Metallics (above) and alcohol (below)

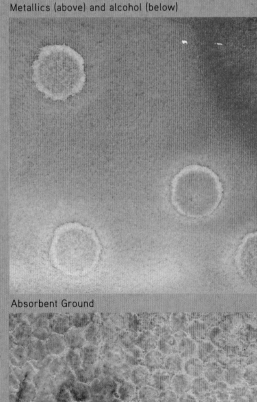

Absorbent Ground

absorbent ground

Another way to get texture in transparent color is with Golden Absorbent Ground. It is similar to gesso but with a less plastic finish. The absorbent finish allows the transparent wash to adhere to it. This technique is great as part of an abstract painting, a page in an altered book, or for textured collage pieces. It can be used on wood, cardboard, and canvas.

1 Take a plastic produce bag that has small air holes in it. Lay it on the paper and paint the Absorbent Ground through the openings of the produce bag. (You can also use stencils to achieve certain shapes.)

2 Remove the produce bag (or stencil) carefully so that you preserve the texture you have made.

3 Allow the Absorbent Ground to dry and then paint over it. I usually use the paint on a brush for this technique because the surface is still a bit slippery. Too much water and the paint will just slide off the surface. The paint will gather in the creases of the texture and darken, while paint on the top will be lighter.

plastic wrap

For a texture that is more geometric, plastic wrap works well.

1 Lay down a wash in a strong color or combination of colors.

2 Next, lay a crumpled piece of plastic wrap on top of your painting, making sure that it is in contact with the wet pigment.

3 Let the painting dry with the plastic wrap in place; this may take 24 hours or more. When you remove the plastic wrap, there will be lines in the wash left by wrinkles in the wrap. These lines can be enhanced with metallic colors or white ink to form more pronounced and decorative abstract shapes.

4 This is a good technique for book covers, collage backgrounds, and cards. For softer lines, remove the plastic wrap before the painting is completely dry. This technique works well as an underpainting. The transparent color that goes over the original texture will allow the texture to show through.

- - - - - - - - - - - - - - - -

tips

➡ To get softer, hazier lines, use waxed paper.

➡ For an ancient textured look, try a combination of burnt sienna, burnt umber, and ultramarine blue.

➡ For a further stretch, spritz on some walnut ink.

➡ To expand your repertoire, fold aluminum foil or waxed paper and press it into your painting. Other options include corrugated paper or bubble wrap, big and small.

➡ Try laying string, burlap, and nylon screening on your background wash.

➡ **CAUTION:** It is very important to wear a dust mask to protect your lungs when working with powders.

➡ Putting the powdered substance in a shaker with large holes (like a pepper shaker) makes application more manageable. Always check to be sure the cover is on securely to avoid a mess.

➡ Be sure to spray the fixative in a well-ventilated area.

rit dye

Another powder technique uses Rit powdered dye.

1 Sprinkle the dye onto dry paper and then spray it with water to help it to stick and dissolve.

2 Pour clear water or light-colored paint over it to help it spread.

3 Let the original wash dry slightly, allowing the powder to settle in a bit. Then add more colors over it.

4 After it is completely dry, brush off the excess powder. This will give you a very textured, almost lumpy, effect—terrific for collage.

5 Spray a fixative over the finished piece.

collage

Collaging with Oriental papers over your watercolor wash is another way to add texture and cover areas. I especially like to use papers with large fibers. When collaged onto the painted surface, the paper becomes translucent and the fibers stay opaque,

Transparent watercolors and calligraphy work well together.

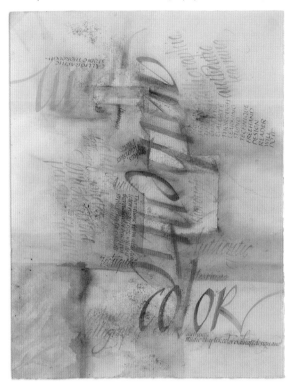

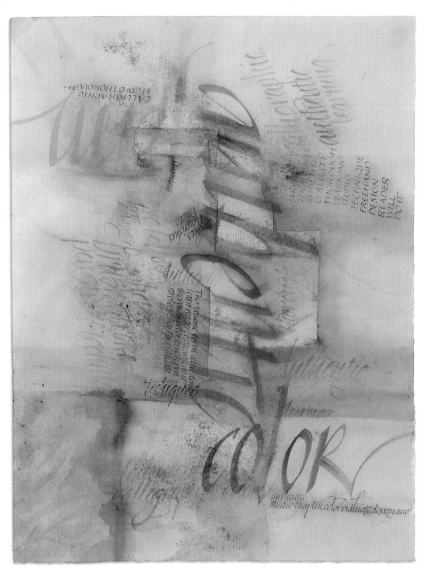

which makes an interesting texture and pattern.

1   Adhere the paper with fluid matte medium. The matte medium is almost invisible and if used thinly enough can be painted over with other transparent colors.

2   On the thinner papers, you can put the medium on top of the paper. The medium will soak through, adhering the thin paper to the base watercolor paper. This technique also works with tissue paper.

As you can see, the possibilities for using transparent watercolors in an experimental manner are practically limitless. Many times the papers created are paintings in themselves. Or perhaps you can put them in a collage box to be cut up later and made into new pieces of art. Make notes in your journal as you move ahead so that you can come back to some of this fun! Play, experiment, and be sure to enjoy the process as well as the product. ✷

BUILDING UPON LAYERS
detailed design made easy

by **beryl taylor**

People often think that my work is very complex, but it's simply created by building upon layers. I make decisions as I go, incorporating a wide variety of materials and methods to create something unexpected from individual components. I would like to share a few of my favorite approaches to creating mixed-media art. None of these techniques is terribly difficult to master; you simply need to work patiently, focusing on each step and each individual layer as you come to it.

INCORPORATE COMMERCIAL FABRICS

Like many other fiber artists, I have a stash of commercial fabrics that I buy because I can't resist their many appealing designs. I find that by creatively incorporating this fabric into my art, I can create original work from readily available fabric. Here are a few simple tricks for using commercial fabric:

Integrate the fabric's pattern into the overall design of the piece. Try placing embellishments in a way that complements the underlying fabric.

Use fabric paints to enhance the original pattern of the fabric by outlining the design or adding corresponding shapes.

Attach a backing to the commercial cotton fabric to make it sturdy enough to be used as the foundation for a mixed-media piece. Felt works particularly well as a backing; I like to handstitch it in place with a running stitch for added texture, but you can also fuse it.

FIND THE BEAUTY IN EVERYDAY OBJECTS

Always keep your eyes open for simple everyday materials that can be transformed into elegant embellishments. With a little tweaking, even mundane items can be beautifully integrated into your art in a few different ways:

Look for inexpensive trinkets at craft stores such as JoAnn Fabrics and Michaels. Apply gesso or metal polish to these bright, gaudy items to give them a more subtle and elegant appearance. You can also paint details onto the pieces, such as gold outlines around the edges.

Check out your local hardware store. Even simple objects such as metal washers will look like fine art if you add them to your piece using decorative stitches and beads.

CREATE A STASH OF EMBELLISHMENTS

I like to make my own embellishments en masse so that I always have some on hand to use in projects as the need arises. I create many different types of embellishments, but these are a few of my favorites:

fabric motifs Machine stitch the outlines of simple shapes, such as circles, through a piece of cotton fabric backed with felt. Cut out these shapes close to the stitching to create motifs that you can attach to a larger piece, layering them if preferred.

paper beads Cut strips of paper into the shape of an elongated triangle. The longer the strip, the fatter the bead will be. Wrap the wide end around a cocktail stick or skewer and roll it up, stopping just before you get to the end and adding a dab of glue to hold the paper in place. You can paint the paper before or after you make the bead.

fabric paper Making fabric paper is a simple and fun way to personalize your mixed-media art. You can apply large pieces of this material to your work or cut out shapes, such as hearts, and attach them with machine stitching to make them pop.

STAMP AND STENCIL

I use quite a bit of stamping and stenciling to add color and pattern to my work in a fairly easy way. Here are a few ideas for including this technique in your art:

➡ Lay sequin waste on top of fabric and use a brush to apply fabric paints through the holes. You can use sequin waste with different-sized holes to achieve multiple circle sizes when stenciling.
➡ Stamp words onto fabric using fabric paints and rubber letter stamps. Make each letter separately, then sew them to the background fabric in order.
➡ Apply modeling paste through a stencil to achieve shapes that have a three-dimensional quality. Once the paste has dried, you can paint the shapes with metallic paints to add some shimmer.

ADD DIMENSION WITH MACHINE STITCHING

I like to include machine stitching in my mixed-media art. You don't have to be particularly experienced in this area to use these simple techniques, and they will add a great deal of visual interest to your work:

➡ Machine stitch around the outlines of individual motifs that you have stenciled or stamped to give them added dimension.
➡ Draw a simple shape, such as a bird, and machine stitch around the outline before filling it in with fabric paint.

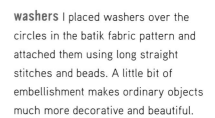

→ Use metallic threads; these will really stand out and add some sparkle to your work.

ENHANCE THE DESIGN WITH HANDSTITCHING

I use handstitching at every stage of the process to add texture and design elements to my work. Here are a few simple ways to get the most interesting results from your handstitching:

→ Use running stitches to attach felt backing to lightweight commercial fabrics; this will give the fabric a raised and textured look that is much more interesting.

→ Add handstitching during the final stages of your work to enhance the overall design. Try creating large, visible straight stitches or adding French knots.

→ Use different colored or variegated threads in contrasting or coordinating colors.

FINISHING TOUCHES

Never underestimate the effect of a few finishing details; even seemingly small additions can truly enrich your work. Here are a few ways to add beautiful final touches to your work:

draw Use ink pens to draw simple designs within images that you have stamped or stenciled.

embellish Add small embellishments, such as beads and sequins, to create textural contrast.

stitch Attach the binding for your piece with visible handstitching and beads for extra embellishment.

washers I placed washers over the circles in the batik fabric pattern and attached them using long straight stitches and beads. A little bit of embellishment makes ordinary objects much more decorative and beautiful.

paper hearts I cut out hearts of fabric paper that I made using gift wrap. I machine stitched them onto the background fabric using metallic thread.

modeling paste flowers I applied modeling paste through a small flower stencil to create raised motifs. Once the paste dried, I painted over the flowers with gold paint.

quilt By using a running stitch to attach felt to the back of this light silk fabric, I added texture to the material and made it sturdy enough to use as a foundation for embellishment. ✳

TEXTURE AND LAYERS
with Acrylic Paint and Stencils

by **lisa kesler**

White Flower on Brown 12" x 12" (30.5 x 30.5 cm)

I used to think of myself as a watercolorist. I had the idea that you were supposed to specialize in a certain technique and label yourself accordingly. But after working for a large collaborative art studio that produced a variety of decorative art for furniture stores, department stores, and interior designers, I quickly let go of my self-imposed label. Provided with all of the materials, supplies, and studio space I needed and a goal to be as innovative as I could, I did a lot of experimenting and began thinking of myself as simply an artist. From that point on, I have enjoyed taking traditional techniques in new directions.

materials

- ☐ Hardboard panel, flat or cradled with sides (I use Ampersand Gessobord; Masonite sealed with gesso is another option.)
- ☐ 3" (7.5 cm) wide masking tape
- ☐ Tracing paper
- ☐ Pencil
- ☐ Graphite stick or very thick, soft-lead pencil
- ☐ Ballpoint pen
- ☐ Craft knife
- ☐ Golden Acrylic Molding Paste
- ☐ Plastic scrapers or small pieces of stiff cardboard
- ☐ Found objects: bits of corrugated cardboard, bottle caps, jar lids, etc.
- ☐ Assorted acrylic paints (I use matte acrylics)
- ☐ Paintbrushes: ¼"–1" (6 mm–2.5 cm) wide, flat
- ☐ Colored artist pencils (I use Prismacolor pencils.)
- ☐ Liquitex Satin Acrylic Varnish

optional

- ☐ Painter's masking tape
- ☐ Palette
- ☐ Brayer

My most recent paintings incorporate a richly textured surface, many layers of paint, simple shapes, and colored-pencil highlights. I love watching the painting take shape as I build up the layers of texture and paint.

PREPARING THE SURFACE

I make my textured paintings on hardboard panels such as Masonite or Gessobord. The hard surface holds up well to the texture I apply.

I like to use Gessobord because it is already primed. If you use an unprimed surface, such as Masonite, it will be necessary to seal it with a few coats of gesso before beginning your painting. If you are using a cradled Gessobord (a board with sides), cover the sides with painter's masking tape to protect them and keep them clean.

APPLYING TEXTURE

1   Completely cover the painting surface with strips of 3" (7.5 cm) masking tape, each strip touching the next so that the entire surface is covered.

2   Using a piece of tracing paper the same size as your surface, make a simple drawing using basic shapes. The shapes can be abstract or realistic, but they should be silhouettes without a lot of detail.

3   Turn the drawing over and trace over the lines on the back with a graphite stick. Flip the drawing back over, so the right side is facing up, and place it on top of the tape-covered surface.

4   With a ballpoint pen, firmly trace over the outlines of a couple of shapes in your drawing. This transfers the outline of these shapes onto the tape-covered painting surface. The rest of the drawing will be transferred later.

5   Cut around the transferred shapes with the craft knife and peel off the background tape around them, leaving the tape shapes still on the surface of the board.

6   Apply the molding paste with a plastic scraper or a strip of cardboard to add texture to the background. It can be applied in

any thickness, but I usually vary the thickness from about ¹⁄₁₆" to ⅛" (2 to 3 mm). Spread the paste over the entire surface using light pressure.

tip: As I drag the scraper across the surface, I am careful to allow some unevenness to remain. I may even leave a few little areas uncoated.

Distant Flight 10" x 20" (25.5 x 51 cm)

7 Stamp a few of your found objects into the surface of the molding paste while it is still wet to add more interest and texture. I like to use a variety of items. These marks will show in the background of the finished painting.

8 Peel up the remaining masking tape, revealing the recessed shapes. Allow this layer to dry completely, 3 to 8 hours, before proceeding.

PAINTING

1 Apply a wash of three or four colors of watered-down acrylic paint over the whole surface with a large brush. This paint layer can be very loose and even sloppy because most of it will be covered up with subsequent layers. Allow it to dry 20 minutes.

2 Choose the main paint color for your background and paint it on. I use a brayer for this step. I place a small dollop of acrylic paint on my palette and roll over it several times in each direction with a printmaking brayer until the brayer is evenly coated with paint. Using large strokes, I roll the brayer over the entire surface to apply an even coat of paint.

3 Reload the brayer (or brush) several times and continue applying paint until you are satisfied with the appearance. This is my favorite step because

White Leaves on Green 10" x 20" (25.5 x 51 cm)

the details of the texture gradually emerge as I roll paint onto the surface. At this point, I can see little bits of the first wash of acrylic colors showing through the texture.

4   After the first color dries, roll on one or two more compatible colors. Each additional layer of color will add to the overall richness of the background. Allow the paint to dry.

MORE TEXTURING

1   Cover the painting surface with strips of masking tape again and transfer the rest of the shapes from your drawing onto the painting surface by tracing over the lines of your drawing as before. Cut these new shapes out with the craft knife, but this time peel up the shapes rather than peeling the tape surrounding the shape.

2   Apply molding paste to the new recessed shapes, being careful not to let the paste seep under the edge of the surrounding masking tape.

3   Peel up the background masking tape to reveal the raised, textured shapes. If any molding paste has seeped under the masking tape to cause irregular edges on these shapes, scrape it off while it is still wet with the tip of the craft knife. Allow the shapes to dry before proceeding.

4   Using a smaller paintbrush, carefully paint the raised shapes with a solid coat of acrylic paint.

If I want the shapes to have the same layered appearance as the background, I mask around the shapes with more tape and then roll on one or two additional colors of paint with a brayer in the same manner used to paint the background, removing the tape once the paint is dry.

FINISHING

1   When the paint is dry, shade and highlight the recessed shapes using colored pencils.

2   Apply a thin, even coat of satin acrylic varnish to the surface to seal and protect it.

Using texture and layers in your acrylic painting, you can create a surface rich with detail, color, and character that no other technique can duplicate. The process and materials become an integral part of the painting. Even with simple shapes and composition, your painting can become a complex brocade of rich surfaces and sumptuous fragments of color. ✳

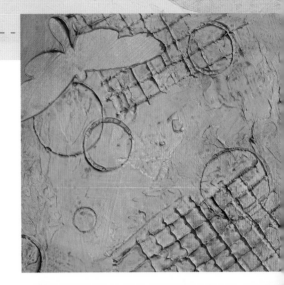

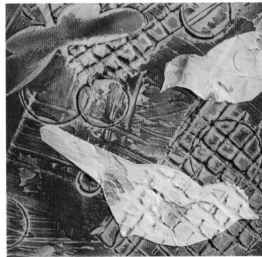

Top: Texture applied with molding paste and a wash of acrylic paint colors.

Middle: The bird shapes were created using stencil shapes cut from masking tape and applying molding paste through the stencil.

Bottom: The bird shapes were painted with a brush and then, using another cut stencil, more paint was rolled on with the brayer.

TRANSLUCENT transfers

by **dj pettitt**

I am always on the lookout for products that have versatile working properties. I was instantly intrigued when I began experimenting with Translucent Liquid Sculpey (TLS) and remained captivated by this adaptable medium. Come along with me to learn these easy techniques and make a simple but beautiful book.

My fascination grew with further experimentation and a desire to create the perfect transfer. I wanted a transfer that was fast and easy with no soaking or rubbing, one that could be made as a stand-alone collage element, and one that could be transferred directly to paper or fabric. The transfer technique that grew from this exploration will add unlimited creativity to your altered books, ATCs, and collage and fiber art.

When making photocopies, I have found that setting the copy machine's contrast a little higher than normal produces better transfers. However, too much contrast will cause the transfer to lose detail and possibly smear when it is heated. If you are unfamiliar with the machine that you are using, experiment with the contrast setting before starting.

tip: Be sure to make copies in reverse (set copier to "mirror").

I have had the best results making transfers with the kind of paper used as deli wrap. Some other papers will work, but keep in mind the following:

→ Silicone-treated parchment paper will work, but the results can vary and will produce a transfer with more of a distressed or aged look. Moisture and steam create wrinkles when parchment paper is heated, causing uneven areas in the finished transfer. There are times when I like this look, but the results are less predictable than with deli wrap.

→ Slick, nonstick surfaces such as heat-resistant craft sheets and the paper backing from iron-on webbing will work well for this technique, too, but will leave the surface of the transfer shiny.

→ Freezer paper or wax paper cannot be used as a nonstick surface for this technique.

MAKING A STAND-ALONE TRANSFER

1   Cut out the image, leaving a small border around the edges.

2   Working on a hard surface, such as a counter, place your photocopied image on a piece of nonstick deli wrap and, depending on the image size, add an appropriate amount of TLS.

materials

- ☐ Black-and-white photocopies
- ☐ Household iron
- ☐ Translucent Liquid Sculpey (TLS)
- ☐ Dry waxed paper or grease-resistant sandwich wrap (deli wrap)
- ☐ Bamboo skewers
- ☐ Fabric scraps
- ☐ Permanent markers (I prefer Faber-Castell Pitt Artist Pens and Y&C FabricMate. You may substitute another favorite marking pen, so long as it is permanent and the ink remains wet long enough for you to blend it.)
- ☐ Soft colored pencils

note: Translucent Liquid Sculpey is a bakeable transfer and color medium available at most hobby/art supply stores. It is nontoxic, but should be used in a well-ventilated room.

Bamboo skewers work well for dispensing and spreading TLS. I find it easier to remove the lid from the bottle and use the skewer to scoop out the TLS than to squeeze it onto the copy.

3   Use your finger to gently spread the TLS outward from the center. (To help remove the paper later, leave a narrow border around the image uncovered and avoid spreading the TLS too thin on the edges.)

4   Begin spreading the TLS in a circular motion, then left to right, top to bottom, until the image is covered. Go slowly and try to keep your finger in contact with the image at all times. Lifting your finger, or moving too quickly as you spread the TLS will trap air in the fluid, creating an undesirable effect.

5   Place a second piece of deli wrap on top of the wet TLS. To help prevent air from getting trapped and creating bubbles in the finished transfer, I apply one edge of the paper and roll it on from left to right. After the top piece is in place, use your fingers to lightly smooth it out and double-check for air pockets.

6   Preheat your iron to high, with no steam. It is very important to cook (cure) the TLS on a hard, heat-resistant surface. Curing on soft surfaces such as towels or an ironing board cover will create air bubbles and uneven holes in the texture and the transfer will tear. To prevent an imprint from the iron when cooking, set the iron on the covered transfer without pressure for a couple of seconds, then lift it up, move it over slightly, and set it down again. Repeat this until the entire image has been set and hardens (this should only take a few seconds). Then add a little pressure to the iron for the remainder of the cooking time to help ensure a nice flat transfer. If you add pressure before the TLS is set, you may get a permanent dent from the side of the iron, or the copy may slide around, making the copy difficult to remove after the transfer is cooked. Use a straight pin to help loosen the edges if this happens. Approximate cooking time using a full-size iron is 15 to 20 seconds for a small image. Irons vary, so you will need to test and get a feel for your iron. To test, lift the corner of the copy and check for pulling and sticking. If the deli paper pulls off easily, it's done.

7   Separate the photocopy and transfer while warm. Waiting too long can result in the copy paper sticking. (The transfer will peel easily from the nonstick deli wrap.) It is important to pull evenly while removing the paper to avoid warping the transfer. If the

transfer sticks and pulls, cook it a bit longer and check again.

8 Apply a pool of TLS on the center front of the photocopy to help lessen the potential for air bubbles. It will take about 1–2 teaspoons of TLS, depending on the size of your image. You need enough to just cover the image: too little, and the transfer will have holes and tear easily, too much TLS will require a longer cook time, and the result will be more opaque.

DIRECT TRANSFERS
sheer fabric

When transferring directly to a sheer fabric, you won't need quite as much TLS as you do when making a stand-alone transfer.

1 Lay a piece of nonstick deli wrap on your work table and place your copy, ink side up, on the deli wrap.

2 Apply TLS to the copy, place the sheer fabric over it, and then add another piece of deli wrap on top. Be sure to smooth out any air bubbles. Heat until cured.

3 Cooking thin and transparent materials on either the front or the back of the transfer, or both, will enrich the layers and add a dreamy quality to the transfers.

4 To add these transparent layers to a cured transfer, spread a thin layer of TLS on the selected areas and place the element on the wet TLS.

5 Cover this with deli wrap and heat until set. Avoid adding a thick coat of TLS directly on top of the image because it will make it somewhat opaque and hide the image when it's heated.

A thin coat of TLS will take only seconds to cure.

tip: Stay away from dimensional items as they prevent the TLS from cooking evenly and your transfer will end up with bubbles and holes.

paper and opaque fabric

You can paint your fabric before or after adding the transfer. If painting first, use diluted textile paint or fabric dye, as regular acrylic paint does not heat well. Let dry, then follow the instructions above for transferring directly to sheer fabric.

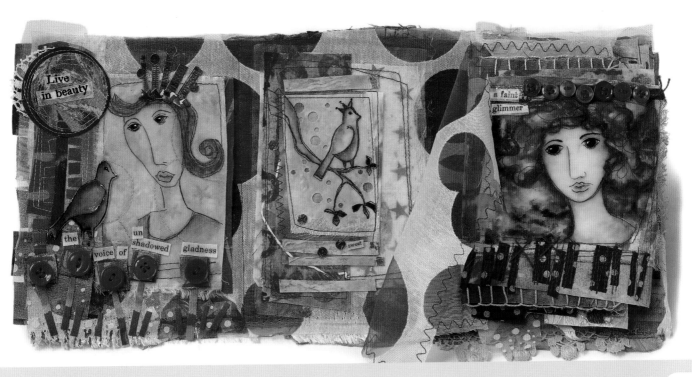

make *the book*

the base

1 Cut one piece of fusible batting 7" × 16" (18 x 40.5 cm) and another piece, 14" × 16" (35.5 x 40.5 cm), from your chosen fabric.

2 Center the fleece on the wrong side of one half of the base fabric and fuse them together following the manufacturer's instructions.

3 Fold the fabric in half, wrong sides together, and pin in place.

4 Bind the edges by hand or machine. Add random free-motion stitching.

decorating the book

I have used a combination of tacky glue, spray glue, clear caulk, and sewing to adhere the layers and collage elements. When adding layers to your book, leave interesting selvedges and raw edges and avoid cutting too straight. Uneven cuts and frayed edges add a whimsical charm. For more dimension and depth, transfers can be sewn on, glued down flat, or layered over lace and glued only around the edges.

creating pockets

Cut a fabric strip 3½" × 10" and press both narrow edges down ½" (1.3 cm). Fold pocket in half and press. Stitch around edges either by hand or machine. Decorate and attach to the page before the page is sewn to the book base.

adding extra pages

Fold a 5½" × 17" (14 x 43 cm) strip of fabric in half to create two pages and bind the edges by machine, or you can apply blanket stitch to the edge by hand. Collage each page as desired. Line up the center fold of the new pages with the center of the book base and sew down this line to attach your pages.

handstitching the book

The layers can get very thick and difficult to handstitch. To help lessen hand fatigue, I use nylon-nose pliers to help pull the needle through the thickness. A small cutting mat will help keep the needle from sliding and help push the needle through.

I like to use size 5 DMC pearl cotton when handstitching. I find that it tangles less than other threads, and I prefer the look of the larger size.

MORE IDEAS FOR LAYERING

embellishments

➡ Feathers

➡ Colored tape

➡ Lace

➡ Buttons

➡ Jewelry

➡ String

➡ Mica

➡ Numbers or shapes cut from
old credit cards

alter transfers

➡ Stamp, sew, and write on the
transfers or use paper punches.

➡ Tear transfers for a more aged and
traditional transfer look.

➡ Leave selected areas uncovered
when applying TLS to the
photocopy. This will create holes
in those areas, exposing the layers
underneath.

➡ Use the transfer as a window in
cards.

quick and easy background techniques

➡ Spread or swirl TLS on your
background (watercolor paper,
muslin, etc.), cover with nonstick
paper, and heat with iron until
cured. Paint or dye background as
desired.

➡ Drizzle and swirl TLS and textile
paint on wax paper and set
aside. Dampen background with

water; lay it on the wax paper
and sandwich between two
nonstick surfaces. Heat with iron
until TLS is cured and paint
is dry. ✳

EXTRA

PAPER ALTERNATIVES ➡

Many artists have discovered the unique properties of these materials and include them in art making. Though they are not paper in the conventional sense, you can use them in many ways that you'd use paper, and they have some additional features that paper does not have.

Tyvek

Tyvek is spun-bonded polythene; you've probably seen it as lightweight white envelopes that feel like plastic. Tyvek will not tear, but cuts easily. It is water resistant, but accepts paints and other coloring agents. Tyvek will shrink, bubble, and distort when heated (use caution when doing so). You can buy Tyvek in sheets or recycle Tyvek envelopes.

Lutradur

Lutradur is 100 percent nonwoven, translucent polyester. You can paint it, stitch it, draw on it, apply heat transfers, and melt or cut into it with a heat tool. When cut, Lutradur does not fray or ravel. Use caution when using a heat tool or burning any material; always work in a well-ventilated area and wear a mask.

Dryer Sheets

Most are made from a nonwoven polyester material coated with a softening agent. They accept paint and ink well and can be easily cut and distorted by pulling.

Color Catcher Sheets

Shout Color Catcher sheets absorb excess dye from fabric during the wash cycle. The colorful used sheets make an excellent material.

MAKING
GELATIN MONOPRINTS

by **jenn mason**

The Lived-in Look, 5½" × 5½" (14 × 14 cm)

the lived in look

f mason 04

I love getting my hands dirty. As a kid I loved Silly Putty and making temporary transfers by pressing it into the Sunday comics. I also loved playing with food, especially making gravy lakes in my mashed potatoes, fanning out apple slices in an apple tart, and watching a Jell-O mold releasing its wiggly wonder. I never tired of the magic. Along the way, as I've grown into an adult artist, I've met others who share my sense of awe in the gooey and gelatinous. And so, I share with you the fun of making gelatin monoprints. A world of beautiful art, fabulous backgrounds, and inspiring collage and quilt additions are just a wiggle away. If you get artist's block from staring at your blank gelatin, try calling in an assistant (preferably under the age of twelve) and watch—there is no better set of artistic jumper cables than watching childlike free play.

materials

- ☐ Unflavored gelatin
- ☐ Water
- ☐ Pyrex or nonstick baking pan
- ☐ Movable surface (cutting board, scrap wood, acrylic sheet, etc.)
- ☐ Brayer
- ☐ Water-based paints or dyes for fabric
- ☐ Paper or fabric
- ☐ Mixing bowl and spoon
- ☐ Microwave or teapot for heating water
- ☐ Cover for work surface
- ☐ Feathers, leaves, found objects, rubber stamps
- ☐ Acrylic or paper palette
- ☐ Newspaper
- ☐ Knife

Overgrown Lawn 4½" × 6" (11.5 x 15 cm)

Gelatin printing can be done on pretty much any surface you can paint on with water-based paints and dyes. There are a number of small variations in the directions, depending on what you are printing and the desired size. I will direct you to the most beginner-friendly way for printing on paper. When printing from a gelatin printing plate, you can either leave the gelatin in a disposable aluminum baking pan or you can use a nonstick baking pan with a smooth bottom and remove the gelatin from the mold onto a movable surface, such as a cutting board, an acrylic sheet, or a plywood scrap. Working in a disposable baking pan

Right: A positive print made by rolling gelatin with multiple colors of fluid acrylics and then pressing and removing a feather from the surface of the plate.

Far right: This print was made after re-rolling the colors from the sample shown above on the gelatin plate surface and then pressing different bottles into the surface and drawing in the paint with a stiff-bristled paintbrush.

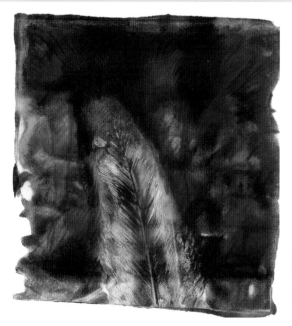

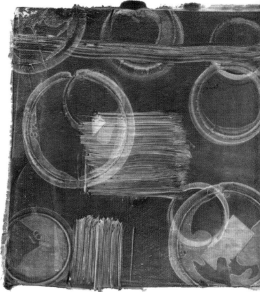

makes clean-up especially easy but doesn't allow you to print off the edge of the gelatin. The directions that follow include the technique of unmolding the gelatin.

➡ Use gelatin in a ratio of 2 tbsp per 1 cup of water (30 ml per 237 ml) to make a firm enough surface to print on.

➡ Gelatin should be ¾" to 1" (2 to 2.5 cm) thick. To determine the amount of gelatin needed, pour water into your molding container to the desired depth and measure the amount of water used.

MAKE A GELATIN PRINTING PLATE

1 In a bowl, mix the unflavored gelatin with half of the water (cold) called for in the package directions, until all lumps are dissolved.

2 Boil the remaining water and add it to the gelatin and water mixture. Stir slowly to keep bubbles from forming.

3 Pour the mixture into the baking pan.

4 Pull torn pieces of newspaper lightly across the gelatin to remove any bubbles remaining on the surface of the gelatin.

5 Let the gelatin sit for 30 minutes and then let it finish setting up in the refrigerator.

6 Remove the gelatin from the refrigerator and let it sit at room temperature for half an hour before using it to print.

7 Fill your sink with hot water. Dip the bottom of the pan into the hot water to melt the gelatin slightly and facilitate removal; unmold it onto your movable surface.

8 Use a knife to cut the gelatin to the desired printing size.

MAKING PRINTS

1 Cover your work surface.

2 Lay down a line of paint on your palette about the width of your brayer and roll the brayer back and forth through the paint until the entire brayer is covered.

3 Roll the brayer over the surface of the gelatin until the desired coverage is achieved.

4 Add small leaves, feathers, flat found objects, or stamp impressions into the paint.

5   Lay a piece of paper over the printing plate and press lightly so that the entire paper comes in contact with the gelatin plate.

6   Carefully pull the sheet of paper up from one corner and set it aside or hang to dry.

positive prints

1   Lay a leaf or a found object on the painted gelatin plate and remove it, leaving an impression.

2   Lay a piece of paper over the plate and press lightly. This makes a positive impression.

negative prints

1   Lay a leaf or a flat found object on a painted gelatin plate.

2   Lay a piece of paper over the plate and the leaf/found object and press lightly. This leaves a negative shape on your print.

ghost prints

Sometimes, enough paint is left on the gelatin plate to make a second impression. Try printing a second paper by either adding or subtracting natural or found elements. You can get an entirely different look by utilizing this ghost-print technique.

experiments

background papers You can create interesting background papers by using the positive or negative methods of printing. You can also paint or stamp directly onto the gelatin. Another fun way of adding texture to a background is by removing paint from the paint-rolled gelatin by pressing different objects into the surface, such as the bottoms of paint bottles (see previous page), Bubble Wrap, crumpled paper, plastic wrap, or other found objects.

found papers While beautiful prints can be made printing on paper and watercolor paper, it is important to consider the opportunities of printing on found papers such as old book pages, sheet music, and maps. By playing with the opacity of the paint, you can alter these papers to create interesting backgrounds, focal points, or future collage elements. You can also print on already printed or woven cloth to alter its appearance.

collages Gelatin printing can be used as a way to either build up a collage on one single piece of paper, or it can be used to create individual collage elements that can later be assembled into a collage (or art quilt, using fabric). ✳

Subtle Domesticity 4½" × 5½" (11.5 x 14 cm)

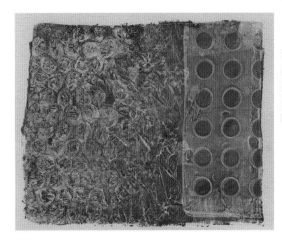

Different items can be pressed or stamped into the surface of the plate before stamping. Left to right: Bubble Wrap, crumpled plastic wrap, and a multi-holed spatula.

ALife OL

in momen

Lovely Figs are everywhere

Je Suis

To Avignon

FIGS

DIOISE

Population Chart
of the Area

à la découverte du pays Diois

		Population	Altitude
H9	Die	4668	410
G10	Espenel	121	370
I12	Establet	21	770
F8	Eygluy-Escoulin	59	600
J9	Glandage	84	860
G12	Gumiane	35	772
H11	Jonchères	36	810
I9	Laval-d'Aix	91	554
J12	Les Prés	25	800
J11	Lesches-en-Diois	33	1020
K10	Lus-la-Croix-Haute	439	1030
H8	Marignac-en-Diois	135	614
I10	Menglon	360	575
J10	Miscon	48	817
H9	Molières-Glandaz	113	520

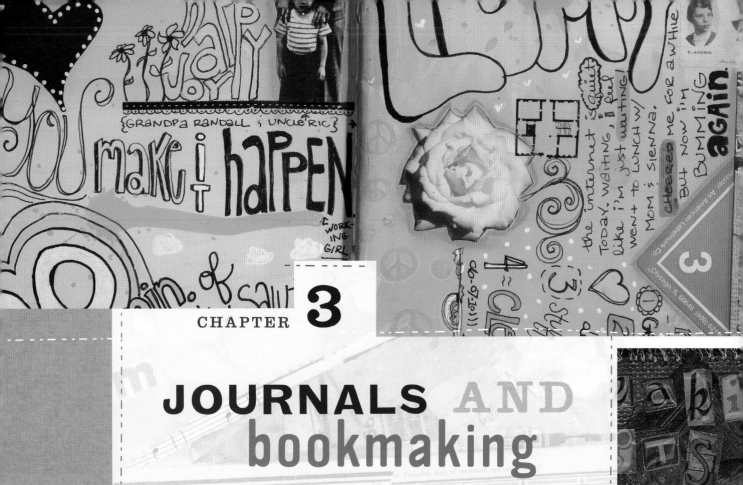

CHAPTER **3**

JOURNALS AND
bookmaking

Journaling is a great way to practice techniques and to create art on a small scale, whether you're jotting down ideas for future art adventures or making individual pieces of art from your journal's pages. Most artists would agree that a journal is a must-have item. In this chapter, artists share not only their art journals, but also their tips for getting started.

KEEPING CREATIVE SKETCHBOOKS

by jane lafazio

As a working artist, I make art to sell and exhibit. But my true passion is not the final product, it's the process. The reason I became an artist is that I like to do creative work with my hands: drawing, painting, collaging, and stitching. Keeping a sketchbook has allowed and encouraged me to make art every day, while enjoying the process of art and creativity and not worrying about the final product.

Daily sketching has helped me improve my drawing and composition skills and has taught me to capture an image quickly. As an artist, it has helped me practice my craft on a daily basis. It's allowed me to experiment with different techniques and compositions by emulating master artists and online artists, trying out their style or color palette.

I spend less than an hour on a sketch or painting, and for those minutes I am totally in the moment. I take the time to sit quietly and really look at an object from my day. It could be something I've picked up on my morning walk or a view from the car while I wait for an appointment. Sometimes I draw in my sketchbook in my studio, other times after dinner, sitting on the sofa with the TV on, or occasionally I perch on my little pack stool on a city street. The point is to stop and capture those moments in a visual diary, chronicling the days, seasons, and activities of my life.

For example, one summer my husband and I spent a lovely weekend in a nearby mountain town. Every morning on the patio of our rented cabin, we would drink our coffee and sketch something from our surroundings. It made the trip so rich and meaningful by having that quiet time each morning to just be.

By observing and drawing in my sketchbook, I've learned that ponderosa pine trees have clumps of three needles and lodgepole pine has two, and that manzanita trees have tiny berries. I've watched a neighborhood tree blossom and fruit through the seasons. I've learned that the crepe myrtle blossoms on the tree in my backyard are made up of tons of tiny berries that burst open to tiny pink petticoat-like blossoms.

I always have two different sketchbooks in progress. One book

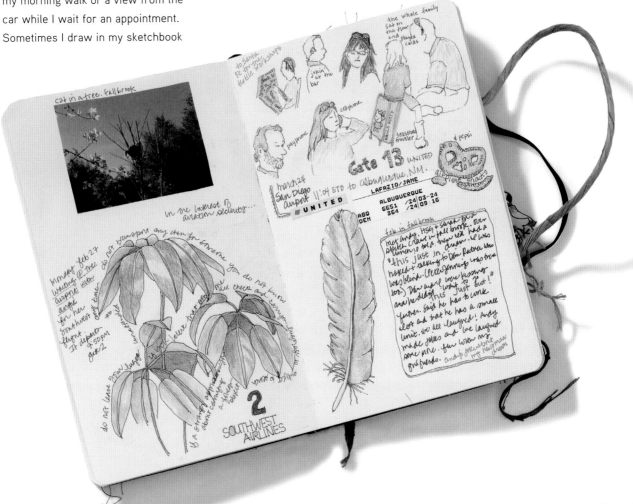

is made of watercolor paper and the other of heavy-duty, acid-free drawing paper. For the drawing paper sketchbook, I use colored pencil and water-soluble crayons to add color to my drawings. I also use the book for collage or more like a scrapbook with ticket stubs or postcards. I often paste in an image from an artist I admire, or even magazine photos of colors that attract me.

As an artist who teaches both elementary school kids and adults, my sketchbooks are a great way for me to try out styles and lessons, and often my own interest in something sparks an idea for a class or project. Of course, my own artwork is influenced by what I've been doing in my sketchbook. My sketchbook is a constant sourcebook of creative ideas.

THE PROCESS

I truly believe everyone can learn to draw; it's all about learning to see—to look really closely—at the object you are drawing. If you are a beginner, start with an apple or another piece of fruit. Look closely at only the outside edge of the fruit. With your pencil, start sketching very slowly by looking at the apple, then at your paper, then at the apple, then your paper, slowly following the outline with your pencil onto your paper. Then, sit back and look at your drawing and the shape of the apple—did you capture every curve? If not, erase those parts and sketch them again. After you've got the outside shape correct, then go in and add the stem or other interior details.

I prefer to draw from the actual subject rather than from a photograph.

my preferred materials

- ☐ Moleskine Large Watercolor Notebook—70 pages (35 leaves) of acid-free watercolor paper with perforated 8¼" x 5" (21 x 12.5 cm) pages.

- ☐ For colored pencil, collage, and water-soluble crayons, I use the Moleskine Large Sketchbook with 100 acid-free, heavyweight pages (50 leaves).

- ☐ Niji waterbrush, medium size

- ☐ I use a plastic palette with various brands of watercolor (Daniel Smith and Winsor & Newton mostly). An inexpensive Prang watercolor student set is fine.

- ☐ Faber-Castell PITT Artists' Pens, superfine tip

- ☐ Pigmented India Ink that is both acid-free and archival, smudge and waterproof when dry

- ☐ Pencil

- ☐ Kneadable eraser

- ☐ Portable folding stool (optional)

what I draw

- ☐ I try to draw something in my sketchbook every day.

I have drawn:

- ☐ Pinecones and pine needles so I can learn the names of pine trees

- ☐ A bunch of flowers from my local farmer's market

- ☐ Paintings or quilts I admired in a museum

- ☐ My kitchen cabinets in the process of refinishing

- ☐ My cats

- ☐ My shoes

- ☐ 14 kindergartener's backpacks

- ☐ Buildings

- ☐ Lakes

- ☐ A radio and a sewing machine

- ☐ My favorite necklace

- ☐ Tubes of paint

- ☐ Pumpkins

- ☐ The contents of my purse

I believe it's better practice for me as an artist, but more importantly it helps me really capture the essence, the detail and shape, of the object. It's a much more immediate experience. Especially if you're drawing a cat, for example, and it moves!

Once I'm happy with the drawing and how it fits on the paper, I use a pen to outline the shapes and refine the detail. The pencil-and-ink drawing takes me anywhere from five to ten minutes, depending on the complexity of the drawing. Then, I fill in the shapes with color. Depending on which sketchbook and the type of paper, I use either watercolor, colored pencils, or water-soluble crayons. I try to exaggerate or enhance the color by using all the colors I see in the object.

Lastly, I add the date and some journaling about my day or what I've drawn. I usually write just a few sentences and let the sketch speak for itself. The journaling makes my sketchbook more than a series of paintings; it becomes my illustrated personal story.

So just get started! Grab a pencil, a scrap of paper, and draw that coffee cup or potted plant in front of you, then write about it. Once you get in the habit, I hope you'll find as much fun and satisfaction as I have. ✸

shape

prickles

still hot today and humid. thunder groans expected. have down chores.

8 inches

after our trip to Idyllwild I decided I should learn the pine, fir + cedar trees in my neighborhood. Brought home this cone with scales that end in sharp prickles and long needles (~8") in bundles of 2 or 3 needles.

2-3 needles

ponderosa pine

commit to a daily walk.

JULY 17

the MEANDER BOOK

by **susie lafond**

I have always adored books and take great pleasure in creating them. The first handmade book I created was a witches' cookbook containing recipes and detailed ingredients lists complete with folded pages. At age eight, I was very proud! Since then I have honed my creative skill using fabric, beads, fibers, and all manner of paper arts to create books. I have always been drawn to things that are not quite what they appear to be at first glance—books with pockets or pullouts, boxes with hidden nooks and crannies. So the idea for sewing pages together in such a way that the book opens in the traditional manner and then has you turning it in a variety of directions—a meander book—was very appealing to me. I enjoy a bit of mystery in art and the sense of surprise it can bring to the viewer.

CONSTRUCTING THE BOOK

1 Cut the pages to your desired size. You will need eight squares total. I chose 4" × 4" (10 × 10 cm) squares for the size and dimension of the pages, but they could be 8" × 8" (20.5 × 20.5 cm) just as easily or any size you want your finished piece to be.

2 If you want painted pages, you need to paint before you sew them together. Use colors that will allow you the most flexibility with the theme you wish to bring to your meander. Let your muse be your guide. Paint each page on both sides, allowing ample drying time for each side. One of my favorite colors is quinacridone nickel azo gold, by Golden. I used a combination of the gold and burnt orange, along with transparent red iron oxide and raw umber.

3 Using a small sponge dipped in paint, dab along the edges of each page for a finishing touch. (I used gold for this.)

4 After your pages have dried, sew them together. Experiment with the width and length of your stitches as this varies by the make and model of the machine. Use scraps for your experimenting rather than your book pages and make sure that the stitches grab both pages as you sew.

5 With the pattern on page 65 as your guide, sew each page together as indicated. Keep in mind that some pages will be sewn on more than one side.

materials

- ☐ Bienfang Canvassette Paper (This is also available under other brand names as canvas paper.)
- ☐ Ruler
- ☐ Scissors and/or rotary cutter and cutting mat. (I prefer a rotary cutter to cut all my pages with accuracy.)
- ☐ Paintbrushes
- ☐ Acrylic paints in your favorite colors (My favorites are Golden quinacridone colors. These are beautifully transparent and allow a layering of colors.)
- ☐ Sewing machine with a zigzag stitch
- ☐ Standard sewing machine needle (You may wish to designate one needle just for sewing your paper arts.)
- ☐ Sewing thread
- ☐ Collage materials of your choice: color copies of photos, decorative and textured papers, pages from old books, old maps
- ☐ Paper glue
- ☐ Relatively flat embellishments and ephemera such as game pieces, buttons, small beads, fibers
- ☐ Small sponge

6 Butt the edges of the first set of pages together. Leave a fraction of an inch between the pages—just enough so they are not quite touching each other. This will prevent the pages from binding when the book is closed. Sew down the length of the two pages. Then lift the presser foot and, reversing the direction of the pages, sew back over the previous stitches. Be sure to reinforce your stitching at both ends of your pages to ensure that the stitches won't loosen with opening and closing your book.

7 Slashed lines on the template indicate where you will add and sew each additional page. You will be sewing pages 1, 2, and 3 together at the sides as indicated. Page 3 is sewn to page 4, and so on as indicated.

8 Once the pages are sewn together, fold the book accordion style. Each fold goes in the opposite direction to the previous one. You now hold in your hands your very own "meander."

PAPER AND FABRIC COMBINATION COLLAGE

The real fun starts now. Gather your favorite collage images, found items, and embellishments. Let your muse go wild. If you are stumped for ideas, it may help to pick a theme for your meander. Your meander could become a unique brag book, a garden journal, or a collection of memories from a summer vacation using items and photos collected and found on your journey. There are no boundaries here.

tip: I have found it is better to stick with rather flat items when choosing embellishments so as not to hinder the book from closing. Small buttons, beads, word tiles, and similar items are all good choices.

1 Start by choosing your papers, fabric, and images for collaging, as well as paper to sew them to. Any decorative paper or textured paper of medium weight will work well for background paper. These items are layered to create each page, as follows: Collage images are sewn to a base piece of decorative or textured paper that is somewhat larger than the images themselves. That piece is then sewn to a layer of lightweight fabric. The final step

additional supplies for paper/fabric collage

☐ Collage images

☐ Decorative and/or textured papers

☐ Lightweight fabrics

☐ Scrap of cardstock or watercolor paper

optional

☐ Small clip

☐ Dritz Fray Check or similar product

meander book pattern

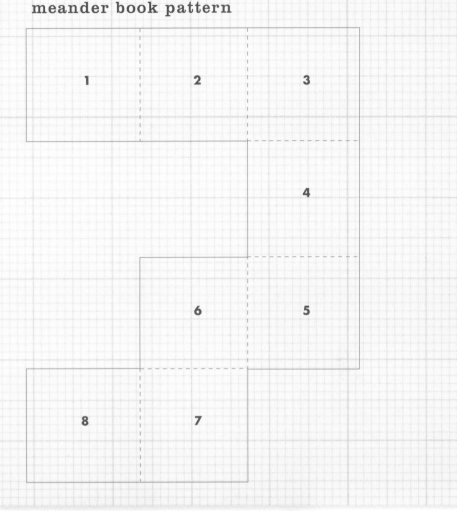

is sewing that to a smaller piece of cardstock or watercolor paper, then gluing your collage to your meander book.

2 Start with your focal images for the collage. Using a small stitch, sew the images to a piece of medium-weight textured paper. This allows the collage images to be securely stabilized before adding the fabric layer.

3 Cut a piece of fabric about 5" (12.5 cm) wider all the way around than the paper you will be sewing it to. Use any kind of lightweight fabric. There are many synthetic fabrics as well as silks and other natural fibers to choose from, many with texture.

tip: The more fabric you allow around the edges of the paper, the more you will be able to scrunch and manipulate the fabric.

4 Take your sewn paper and fabric to the sewing machine. Center the paper on top of the fabric. Lay both pieces under your sewing machine's presser foot and put the needle in the down position so it pierces through both paper and fabric, which will serve as an anchor as you begin sewing. Before you begin sewing, scrunch up the fabric a bit so you create some texture as you sew. Sew using a ¼" (6 mm) seam allowance from the edge of the paper. Continue to bunch and scrunch the fabric as you sew

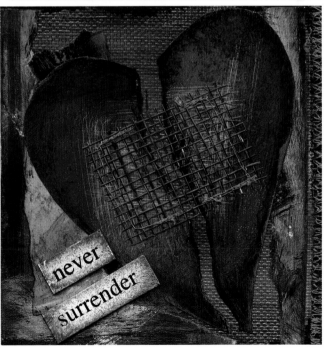

until you go all the way around to where you began.

5 Once you have sewn all the way around your piece, remove it from the sewing machine and cut off any loose threads.

6 Add a base layer of sturdy cardstock. This will sandwich the fabric in the middle. This will give you a bonding surface so you can use it on your artwork without needing to actually apply glue to the back of the fabric. I chose a 4" × 4" (10 × 10 cm) scrap of watercolor paper. Any scrap will work. Center this piece so that it matches up with the paper on top of the fabric layer. Use a small clip to hold it all together when you take it to the sewing machine.

7 Place the piece on your sewing machine and simply sew following the edges of the paper on the top of the fabric, being careful to catch the paper underneath the fabric. You will be sewing blind at this point, so careful placement is important. I purposely sewed around more than once, allowing the stitching to be less than perfect.

8 If you are working with fabric that has a tendency to fray or ravel, apply Fray Check, using a small amount on a cotton swab and dabbing around the edges of the fabric.

9 Embellish further with ephemera, beads, charms, and buttons.

tip: When sewing paper and fabric, always sew from the top of your piece. If you turn the piece over to sew on the opposite side, the needle punches the paper outward, and it will show on the finished side. ✳

EXTRA

EASY BOOKBINDING →

The binding you select for your handmade book or journal can be simple or elaborate, with many choices in between. Choosing just the right string, thread, or fiber to stitch the binding with can add a lot to your creation. Here is a simple binding to get you started.

Pamphlet Stitch

1   Assemble your pages. Using the pencil and ruler, mark three holes, evenly spaced, along the spine. Punch the holes using an awl (**fig. 1**).

2   With the signature opened flat, thread the length of thread, yarn, ribbon, or string through the center hole (a) from the outside, leaving a 4" (10 cm) tail on the outside. Go back out through the top hole (c), and then back in through the bottom hole (b), bypassing the center hole (**fig. 2**).

3   Thread the string back through the center hole (a) to the outside and, using the two tails, tie the string around the long string running from the top hole to the bottom hole. Tighten and tie off (**fig. 3**).

4   Add beads, fibers, and charms to the tails, if desired, or trim the tails close to the book with scissors.

materials

☐ Prepared book pages, folded

☐ Length of waxed linen thread, narrow ribbon, yarn, or string, 3 to 4 times the height of the book

optional

☐ beads, fibers, charms

tools

☐ Pencil

☐ Ruler

☐ Awl

☐ Heavy needle with an eye large enough for your thread or string

☐ Scissors

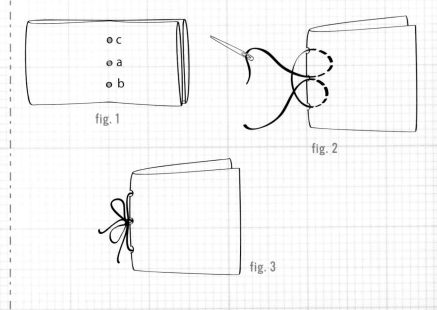

fig. 1

fig. 2

fig. 3

art journaling
PAGES *in* STAGES

by **dawn devries sokol**

Four years ago, I decided I wanted to art journal, but I had difficulty beginning. My desire to art journal led me to various blogs and websites, seeking journal pages to inspire me and get me started. I also found art books filled with invaluable tips and techniques, but I didn't find anything to help me get past the blank page.

I attended workshops with incredible teachers explaining their methods, and their hands-on instruction answered my technique questions. But I still had nagging doubts when I attempted to art journal on my own. What was I supposed to journal about? How should I start? How do I art journal a whole page in one sitting?

In workshops, I had observed students effortlessly whipping up journal page after journal page, while I was at a standstill. Deflated, I knew that even if I were willing to sit down with my journal, it didn't necessarily mean I would actually finish a page, or even make a mark. I kept hitting a roadblock, and I couldn't bear it any longer.

Then, I had an epiphany: I realized I needed to listen to my creative intuition. I was unnecessarily pressuring myself to complete a journal page in one sitting. I realized it didn't matter what other artists did. There are no rules in art making, so why was I looking for rules to guide my art journaling?

I needed to let my art journal pages develop slowly. I had to understand and accept that what worked for others wasn't necessarily going to work for me, and that would require patience.

I started to art journal when I felt like it, using the technique that inspired me at that moment. I painted in my journal some days and collaged, doodled, or wrote in it on others—using the same or different pages. I didn't worry about chronological order or creating pages focused on one subject or idea. I learned which techniques worked for me and which didn't. I gave myself permission to paint over pages I didn't like, and I painted and collaged over pages that contained writing and doodling. Suddenly, as the rules vanished, so did my inhibitions. I was journaling—on my own terms—and loving it.

Working on my journal pages in stages is key to my art-journaling process. If you're having trouble getting started in your journal, you may want to try this no-holds-barred approach.

There are three stages I like to work in:

→ Painting

→ Collage

→ Doodling and/or writing

PAINTING

1 Flip through your art journal and stop at whatever page speaks to you.

2 Pull out a couple of paints and squirt one of the colors in

materials

☐ Fabriano Artistico watercolor paper, 140 lb hot-pressed, for making handmade journals

☐ Inexpensive fluid acrylic paints, such as Delta Creative Ceramcoat or Plaid Apple Barrel

☐ Paper towels

☐ Various household items for creating lines, texture, etc.

dime- to quarter-sized spots, here and there, on your page. I like to use combinations of chartreuse green and light blue, pink and orange, or sometimes red and teal.

3 Choose another color and apply it in the same way. Using your fingers, rub the paints in, combining the colors. Make sure to cover the whole page. If you have empty areas, squirt a little more color onto the page and rub it in.

tip: I spread paints with my fingers because it leaves a smooth finish on the page, the paints blend better, and I feel like I have more control.

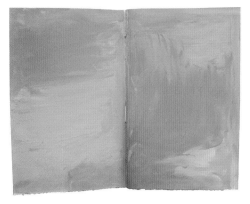

Journal pages with painted background.

4 Paint about five pages in one sitting; do more or less if you want. Listen to your instincts and stop when you feel like it.

change it up

→ Use a paintbrush with tough bristles to add a lined texture to your backgrounds.

→ Water down your paints for a wash across your pages. Have plenty of paper towels on hand to blot up excess paint.

→ Use paper towels to create a different look. Spread the paint across a page, let it dry slightly, and then wipe the paper towel across the page, removing some of the wet paint. Try this method with baby wipes for a slightly different effect.

→ Apply paint with items such as sponges, old credit cards or hotel room keys, combs, etc., to create different textures.

Working in stages allows your mind to work more freely while creating. It will be easier to start each stage because you'll work according to how you are inspired at any given time. I let my creative mood take over and I do what I want. Remember, no rules, no worries. That's what art journaling should be about.

COLLAGE

Collecting collage fodder can be an ongoing activity. Flip through old magazines and cut or rip out anything that pleases you. This can include words, objects, and/or patterns. Turn the magazine upside-down to see images in a different way. Keep a basket or folder (or many) to throw bits into when you find them. Think about having an envelope in your purse to store everyday items from your travels: straws and candy wrappers, coffee cups, printed napkins, receipts, decorative tape, stickers, etc.

Remember, you can work in any stage in any order, but it's important to work in the stage that best fits your mood.

1 Open your journal to a painted page. The conversation may begin with the color palette you've chosen or the way the color appears on the page. Whatever it is, don't think too much about it.

2 Sort through your collage stash for images that appeal to you. Keep your journal close by and open to the page you intend to play on.

3 Select several images in various sizes and other collage bits that may work color-wise. I suggest five to ten items. I like using black-and-white images for their contrast against my bright backgrounds.

4 Cut out and place the images on your page. Don't think about placement too much. I've found that overthinking makes me hesitant in my choices. Include a large image to create a focal point. This balances the page and makes it more aesthetically pleasing.

5 Once you are happy with your arrangement, attach the collage bits. Mono Adhesive is my first choice, but I use gel medium when placing images that I plan to paint over because it keeps the images smooth and stable. Clear tape or any of the decorative tapes will provide some added interest, too.

Listen to your intuition when it tells you to stop. Remember, you can always add more collaged bits later or paint over things. It's your art journal; there are no rules.

- - - - - - - - - - - - - -

try these ideas

→ Create new images on the page out of your collage bits.

→ Collage borders on your pages.

→ Combine some found pieces of ephemera with photos you've taken.

→ Insert images with personal meaning. I often use photographs I've shot.

→ Repeat images. Some journal artists photocopy their pages, cut them up, and include these images in their collages.

→ Cut up photos and other bits. You don't have to use full images. Cut a person in half and place them right on the edge of your page, so it looks like they're looking in. If you have a group photo, cut out certain

people and scatter them across the page.

➡ Add depth to your collage with transparencies. Anytime I find clear wrappers with text or an image on transparent paper, I stash it. You can also use clear packing tape and black-and-white photocopies to create great little transparencies.

little things mean a lot

Add small touches for enhancement and depth during any stage.

Ink splotches I love to use inks to add splats on pages.

Crayon lines Color around the edges of the pages.

Photocopies Adhere high-contrast black-and-white photocopies with gel medium. When dry, brush a light, watered-down acrylic over them to match the background, so they blend into the page.

Tissue paper I've adhered thin tissue with gel medium at every stage.

Words Label makers are a good way to paste words to your page.

Rubber stamps Use ink that is slightly darker than your background paint. Journal or doodle over it.

WRITING AND DOODLING

For me, doodling and writing is the most mobile of the three stages. When I travel, I prep my journal before the trip. I paint and collage on the pages and leave them to be doodled and written upon while I travel. I may add

some collage on the road, but mostly I just doodle and journal. This allows me to pack fewer supplies, and that works very well for me.

doodle it up

With your paint and collage images already on the page, start to doodle. I use anything that's in my arsenal. Doodling can be mindless or meditative. It can also be a thoughtful form of expression. Sometimes I brainstorm while I doodle.

If you're struggling to start, here are some tips:

→ Think of shapes. I like hearts, flowers, stars, circles, rounded squares, swirls, and all kinds of flourishes. Shapes are easy to repeat and they fuel the doodling process.

→ Outline or color one of the collage images to make it really pop off the page.

→ Create animals, creatures, or flowers from ink or paint splatters.

→ Doodle with markers a little darker than your background paint. These can be written over later with a darker or white pen, if you wish.

→ Continue the lines of any shapes or collage images you added.

→ Start at the edge of your page and doodle a simple border of dashed lines, triangles, flowers, etc. Continue to add to the border with other shapes, as desired.

→ Section off a corner of your page, then doodle within it. Sometimes

this helps when you feel overwhelmed by all the space on your page.

→ Look through a magazine or book containing endless patterns and prints to spark your doodle energy.

→ Try not to be linear in your doodling. Flip your journal upside down and doodle that way, too. Sometimes you have to rotate your page to think beyond the ordinary. Doodle across your page at all sorts of angles.

word it up

While doodling shapes, patterns, and lines, I also doodle words. Words that I doodle large are usually phrases that strike me, the title of a song that I'm listening to, or a movie quote I just can't get out of my head. Putting on

some headphones and listening to music that makes me groove really helps me during this stage.

You can write about anything in your art journal. Try words that pop into your head throughout the day, or words from a song that won't leave you alone. Make lists, jot down random thoughts, record the things you need to do, etc. You don't need to fill your page with doodles and journaling all in one sitting; journal random doodles and words as they occur to you. Date these entries, if you wish, for documentation.

To conquer a writing roadblock, try some of these strategies:

→ Draw some wavy lines on your page and use them as a guide. You can pencil them in and erase later, or make them a part of your

design. I did this when I started journaling and this practice has increased my confidence in my writing and lettering.

→ Trace letters from stencils for larger words and then fill them in with color. Add flourishes.

→ Rubber stamp words and then fill them in with pens that match the color of the ink pad. Draw in flourishes, if you like.

→ Cut out a large word from a magazine. Extract the letters completely from the background with a craft knife and glue the letters onto the page. Doodle within the words and/or add flourishes and other lines flowing from them.

Listen to your gut when it tells you to stop. There is no rule stating that pages can't be left unfinished. You can always paint, collage, or doodle more later. Go back to these pages when you feel the groove.

Remember to mix and combine these stages to work for you. If you want to collage first, then paint, then doodle and journal, do it! If you want to write on the page and then cover it with paint and collage, then write some more, try it. Open your mind, set yourself free, and your art journal will work for you. ✳

TRAVEL journals
maps as a starting point

by jacqueline newbold

Sitting in the cozy kitchen of a seventeenth-century stone cottage in the tiny hamlet of Campagnac, I pull out a map of southern France. It unfolds to fill up the entire kitchen table. With my chin in my hands, I lean over to locate the path of my journey for the past week. The tangible feel of the map inspires me to run my fingers along meandering ocher and cerulean lines and roadways, dotted and dashed.

I am immersed in the French country-side where the honey-colored stone walls glow with the warmth of long autumn days. Here, the warm breeze encourages the fall of tasty ripe figs from the gnarled trees. The ancient, perched villages beg for exploration as we drive down narrow lanes lined with tall straight plane trees, planted long ago to give shade to Napoleon's marching army. Here in the cottage, I am giddy with artistic joy as I have time to paint in my watercolor journal, my constant travel companion.

I am fascinated by maps. I love the fact that they represent where I have been and give direction to where I may go. I love the excitement of finding my way amongst exotic sounding villages—Blauzac, Sainte-Anastasie, Châtillon-en-Diois, and Ponet—not knowing what scenery will appear around the next turn.

While experimenting with ways to incorporate maps into my watercolor journals, I discovered that they create interesting and mysterious textured backgrounds for watercolor paintings. Maps also make a great foundation for mixed-media collage, collected ephemera, and journaling. Or, using a published map as my guide, I'll draw my own map of an area, lightly paint over it with a wash of watercolor, and then add little drawings to represent the local charm.

Taking the time to sketch and paint a map, or using a map as the background for my art, imprints in my mind the stunning and colorful locations found along my journey. For example, the map I painted while camping at Big Summit Prairie, Oregon, will always bring back the splendor of the seemingly never-ending, dazzling white fields of mule's ears in bloom, sprinkled with specks of wildflower colors. Whether you are painting a charming European village or journaling about the sparkle of an ocean wave, using a map as the starting point for your art will bring back fond memories of your voyages for years to come.

DIRECTIONS

1   Cut or tear the map into an interesting shape that will fit in your journal.

2   Drizzle a little bit of white gesso onto the map and quickly spread it out with a paper towel, before it starts to dry. Rub some of the gesso off so that the map shows through but has a slightly pushed-back look. Allow to dry.

tip: The gesso dries quickly, so if your map piece is large, work in small areas, one area at a time. Ideally, you want the map to look whitewashed, with the map showing through in some areas more than others.

1   Paint a colorful wash using watercolor paints. Try a mix of colors that are close to each other on the color wheel, such as magenta, rose, and quinacridone gold. Transparent watercolor paints will let parts of the map show through. Allow the watercolor to puddle and bead up to create interesting effects. Try not to use too much water; let the

materials

- ☐ Map or a color copy of a map (Make sure the ink on the copy is not water soluble.)
- ☐ White gesso (Liquitex or Golden Artist Colors)
- ☐ Paper towels
- ☐ Watercolors (I use Winsor & Newton and Daniel Smith watercolors.)
- ☐ Watercolor brushes (I like Daniel Smith Platinum series, round sizes 4, 8, and round mop #6.)
- ☐ Pencil
- ☐ Permanent black ink pen
- ☐ Glue

optional

- ☐ Stamps and ink pads for creating a border

paints mingle and blend on their own. Allow to dry.

2 Using a pencil, draw the image you want to paint, such as a European perched village scene, a grove of olive trees, or wildflowers in the foreground.

3 Paint in houses, trees, and distant hills using a variety of colors. Allow to dry.

4 Outline the drawn images and some accents with a permanent black pen.

5 Paint a page in your journal with watercolors, let it dry, and then glue your map art to it.

6 Stamp along the edges of the map to create an interesting border or simply outline the outer edge of the map with a pen.

Opposite: A map is the background for this painting. Flowers were painted, cut out of watercolor paper, and adhered to the foreground to add texture and depth.

Below: A watercolor sketch enhanced with a map, decorative papers, labels, magazine images, stamping, text, and journaling.

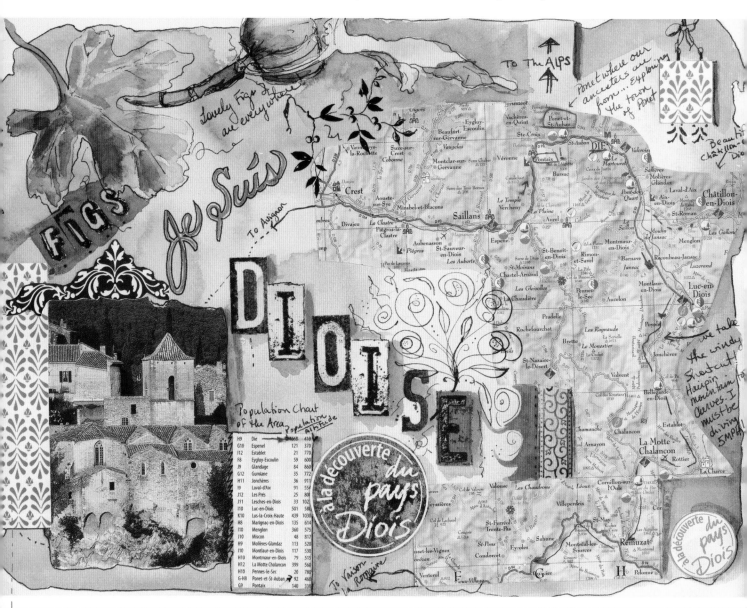

ideas for using maps

➡ Make copies of maps and prepare them with gesso before you leave on your trip.

➡ Make a hand-drawn map of the area you are visiting and incorporate little drawings of interesting points along the way.

➡ Use a map as a starting point and add collected ephemera such as business cards, tickets, postage stamps, cut-out words and photos from brochures, wine labels, paper money, paper napkins, postcards, and anything else that catches your eye.

➡ Use a map as a foundation for your journaling.

➡ Cut a map into interesting shapes that can be folded out from the page to reveal your art.

➡ Use different types of maps for different looks, such as nautical charts for marine scenes or hiking trail guides for nature paintings. ✳

IF THESE WALLS COULD TALK
home journaling

by **lynn whipple**

As a mixed-media artist, I have always been fascinated by old books, history, and odd bits of memorabilia. The idea for my own "Home Journal" came from my desire to take my collaged pages and make something three-dimensional. You can transform your own treasures into a standing house using collage, drawing, painting, sewing, journaling, and embellishing. Follow the directions here to make your own home journal, which will stand up beautifully and store flat just as easily. You can even display it without the roof, folded out like an accordion. Your finished home will be about 7" x 12" (18 x 30.5 cm). Use all of your creative talent to build your dream house.

CONSTRUCTING YOUR HOME JOURNAL

Start your home journal by cutting your canvas paper into shapes to construct your house: four sides, two roof peaks, one roof.

1 Measure and mark the four side wall shapes on the canvas paper with your ruler and pencil. Each side wall should be 4" x 6" (10 x 15 cm). Cut out with your scissors and set aside.

2 Mark on the canvas paper and cut out two triangles for your roof peaks, each 4" (10 cm) on the bottom and 3⅜" (7.7 cm) on the sides. If you measure from the bottom center of the triangle to the top point, it should measure 2⅜" (5.7 cm). Cut out with scissors and set aside.

3 For your roof shape, draw a rectangle on your canvas paper that is 7" x 5" (18 x 12.5 cm). Cut out with scissors. Fold this in half, bending the 7" (18 cm)

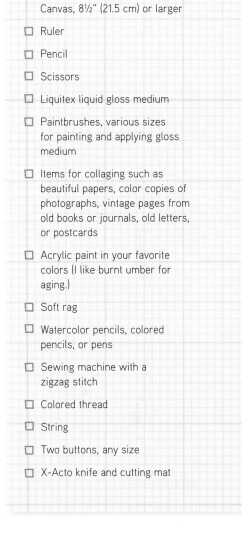

materials

- ☐ Bienfang Canvassette Heavy Paper Canvas, 8½" (21.5 cm) or larger
- ☐ Ruler
- ☐ Pencil
- ☐ Scissors
- ☐ Liquitex liquid gloss medium
- ☐ Paintbrushes, various sizes for painting and applying gloss medium
- ☐ Items for collaging such as beautiful papers, color copies of photographs, vintage pages from old books or journals, old letters, or postcards
- ☐ Acrylic paint in your favorite colors (I like burnt umber for aging.)
- ☐ Soft rag
- ☐ Watercolor pencils, colored pencils, or pens
- ☐ Sewing machine with a zigzag stitch
- ☐ Colored thread
- ☐ String
- ☐ Two buttons, any size
- ☐ X-Acto knife and cutting mat

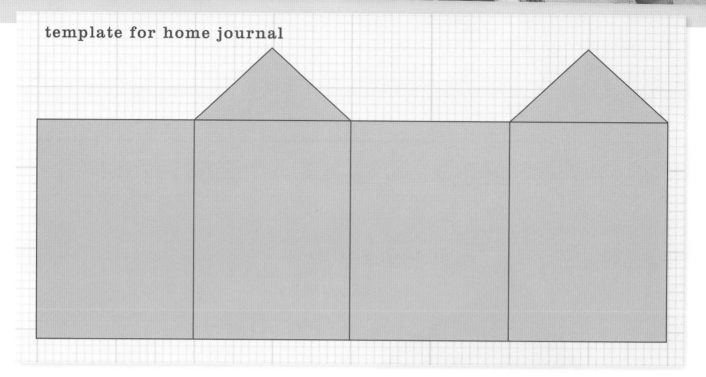

template for home journal

side in the middle. Then mark two flaps in the roof, each flap a three-sided rectangle that is 1" × 1" × 2" (2.5 × 2.5 × 5 cm). Center these rectangles in the middle of each pitch of the roof. Cut out the shapes. Bend the flaps out just a little so you can see inside the house.

talking walls

Now comes the fun part—covering your "walls" using all your creative energies. Communicate your ideas by building a story and a surface. Try something new, layer, follow your desires, trust your voice. If you don't like something, do what I do—just build up another layer on top of it. This is where the good stuff happens.

I strongly recommend you trust your own personal design preferences.

There is no wrong way, and that is where the joy comes in. Here are the steps I followed, but feel free to take artistic license.

1   Begin a collage on one of the side walls by using gloss medium to glue some interesting paper down, perhaps an old letter or postcard. Let this dry.

2   Dilute acrylic burnt umber paint with a little water and lightly spread it over the surface of the canvas paper. Blot the canvas with a soft rag and wipe it to remove as much color as necessary to make your collage look aged.

3   Look for an interesting image and collage it on top. This is the beginning of your storytelling. As you layer and add to your collage, an idea will surface that will begin to drive your narrative.

4   When you have finished collaging the outside, work on the inside so it's interesting to look at through the flap openings.

it's time to sew

1   To start the construction of your home, take two sides and butt them together. Sew them together by machine using a zigzag stitch. Have your zigzag stitching cross over, back and forth, over each piece. Keep your overall design and story in mind while sewing so that the walls are attached in the correct order. Backstitch at the beginning and at the end.

2   Attach the next two sides in the same manner.

3   On the fourth side, do not attach it to another side but simply run the stitching along the edge so it

Inside walls of *Silly Men*.

looks the same as the others. Then fasten a button on each open side; on the side opposite each button, attach some string to wrap around the buttons to make a simple closure. The great thing about stitching in this manner is that the house will fold easily and stand up as well.

4 Now sew the two roof peaks to the top of two walls that are opposite each other, again using a zigzag stitch.

5 Choose a solid color for the roof and paint both the top and the underside. When dry, decorate the top with pen or colored pencil. Embellish as desired.

6 Set the roof on top of the standing house and you have finished your own home journal. Enjoy! ✷

CHAPTER 4

COLLAGE AND assemblage

Artists have shown that there is no limit to the kind of items you can include in collage. They have even enlisted the help of their computers! In this chapter, artists show how to add amazing texture and meaning to your collages in a variety of ways. And if collage is not your thing, take a look at how some of our favorite artists take everyday castoffs and finds to create one-of-a-kind assemblages.

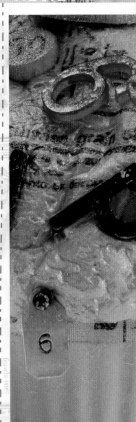

STOP LOOK! *listen*
recycling your world into art

by **the oiseaux sisters**
susan andrews and carolyn fellman

Green studios: recycling, reusing, and zero waste. It sounds serious and sensible, and it is. Do it: it's good for you. Working green can be an act of pure creative delight, and zero waste is extremely satisfying. What do we mean by zero waste? It is a way of living and working that attempts to conserve resources, avoid waste, and consciously assign the most appropriate end use to every material object that enters your life. The challenge here is to wind up with the tiniest possible contribution to the waste stream.

Sewing Sisters
4" × 4½" × 6¾"
(10 x 11.5 x 17 cm)

The Secret of Happiness/Paint Tube Babies 9" × 10¾" (23 × 27.5 cm)

REIMAGINE FOUND OBJECTS

Start by simply paying attention. Try reimagining another use for almost everything you use as a lifelong practice. Is it art? Is it useful? Is it necessary? Can it be recycled by me or others? If you already work with found objects, you are very familiar with reimagining. Found object (recycled/altered/trash) art is not so much about technique. It's a worldview—a way of seeing. Turn your mind to reimagining what you're looking at, and it is the world itself that is altered and art will follow. It is the artist's job to try to meet each new day and environment with fresh eyes, to find what attracts, disturbs, amuses, enlightens: to see the eccentric little corner of the view that everyone else misses.

Chances are, if you have found your way to these pages, you already take pleasure in collecting, arranging, and rearranging all sorts of things. You know the charms of found objects—a dented pot lid, a bit of driftwood or seashell, a flattened can or bottle cap, a root, a feather. With eyes wide open, you roam the world's rummage sales, beaches, forests, gardens, and parking lots imagining

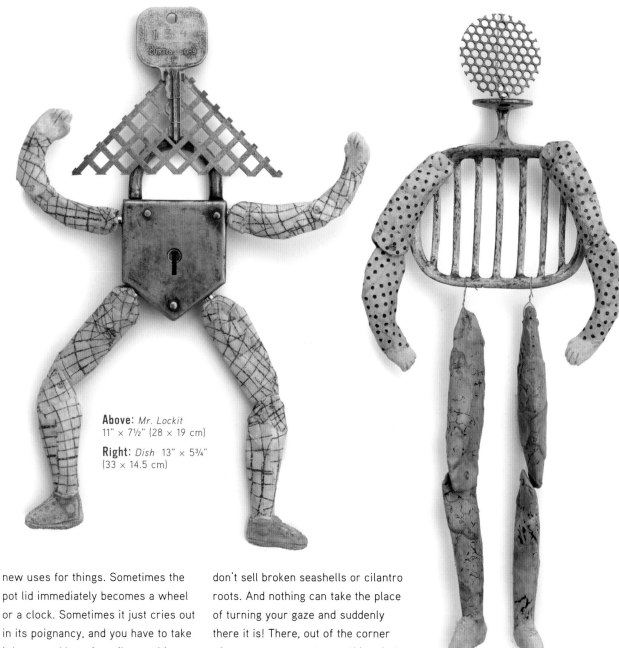

Above: *Mr. Lockit*
11" × 7½" (28 × 19 cm)

Right: *Dish* 13" × 5¾"
(33 × 14.5 cm)

new uses for things. Sometimes the pot lid immediately becomes a wheel or a clock. Sometimes it just cries out in its poignancy, and you have to take it home and keep it until something occurs, and it becomes a piece of art.

Of course you can find all sorts of boxes and pot lids and shells at craft supply and dollar stores. You can buy old things and found objects on eBay and other websites, too. But they don't sell broken seashells or cilantro roots. And nothing can take the place of turning your gaze and suddenly there it is! There, out of the corner of your eye, you spot something that changes your work and gives you a whole new perspective on what you want to make. Sometimes it is the very abandonment of certain objects that sparks creativity and urges the hapless artist toward adaptation.

IS IT REALLY JUNK?

Now try to reimagine some of the less inherently appealing junk that finds its way into your life. Unlike found objects that are well-hunted and loved, empty containers, packaging, junk mail, and other plastic detritus accumulates around every modern life, whether it is wanted or not. Trying to use everything that comes your way is certainly a huge creative challenge. Before it overwhelms you, start paying more attention to what you allow in. Consider shopping more carefully to cut down on packaging or shop in a watchful way to acquire packaging you find appealing and useful.

Once you acquire something, however, really consider the possibilities before tossing it in the trash or recycle bin. Can you find a way to take advantage of the very nice paper in that catalog? Can this molded plastic bubble pack be cast with papier-mâché or plaster and turned into an appealing form? Can those plastic bottle lids become a handy way to store small quantities of paint? The answer to all of these questions is a resounding yes. The reimagining here may be a bit pragmatic and prosaic, but it can have a huge impact on how you organize your studio and do your work.

So, what is useful and what is waste? Most of us are quite overwhelmed with the amount of stuff that accumulates around our lives, our homes, our studios. Storage is always a concern, and you can't keep everything. However, there are some simple steps you can take to tame the mess, save time, conserve supplies, and jump-start your studio explorations.

OUR ZERO-WASTE PRACTICES

We live and work year-round in garden studios. By accident or by design, natural elements frequently creep into our work. During the winter months we scavenge the Mexican Gulf shores for feathers, sea glass, shells, and curious storm-stranded debris. Susan's *Shell Seekers/Tide Zones* (page 89) is an ongoing series of carved scrap wood and Paperclay sculpted figures incorporating such treasures. These small worn shell souls speak to how we become what we love.

Summers we prune and print the veined leaf beauty that abounds in our upstate New York gardens. *Spectator* is part of a papier-mâché shoe series made in tribute to Susan's stylish gardening mother. It was inspired by the gift of a robust cilantro root left on our porch by a market gardener friend. A burdock leaf was inked and printed to pattern the paper. A real shoe was used as the mold for casting.

Today, you can recycle most paper. But when Susan started making altered books and mixed-media paper dolls, there was no such recycling. She started sawing books and wood scraps on the band saw to create her *Little Librarian* series. She uses these books in the paint studio to paint out her brushes before rinsing them in water.

Spectator 9½" × 3" (24 × 7.5 cm), with a 5½" (14 cm) heel

In time, the rippled and paint-stained pages accrue the soft, worn quality of a beloved, oft-read book.

Most of the wood we use is scavenged from the trash. We keep an eager eye on all construction projects in our neighborhood. These are also a good source of metal, such as scraps of aluminum, copper flashing, screening, and other interesting debris. The camel in *Overland* combines paint sludge from the bottom of the can with Dumpster pine scrap. The legs are twigs with feet left over from a stuffed cloth doll. Body and legs are wound in thread, painted over with medium, and embellished with buttons from a flea market sewing basket.

As you can easily see, found objects inspire and animate all of our work in one way or another. We have large collections sorted and stored in baskets and bins, suitcases and shelves, and all manner of storage systems. There are usually several lovely pieces of trash furniture genteelly aging out in a corner of our yard.

RECYCLED HISTORY

We also recycle our own art history. When sketching a new piece in the studio, we will often cannibalize old work and use parts we've made before in a new way. This revision and reinvention gives us a little momentum that is enhanced by putting some found objects into the mix. *Dish* and *Mr. Lockit* (page 86) came together by trying previously made papier-mâché doll parts with some treasures a friend scavenged and gave us.

Carolyn finds clocks a very satisfying end product for some of our collection of kitchen cast-offs. For the clock shown below, the base disk (in this case, a piece from some sort of canning apparatus) was pounded on an anvil to shape and flatten the edges. The numbers were stamped with a half-inch, metal alphabet stamp set. It was then scoured, sanded, and tinted very slightly with transparent acrylic paint along with the percolator basket lid centerpiece. A precision quartz clockwork holds the pieces together. The hands were beaten on an anvil as well and then painted.

We love to wander flea markets, and sewing baskets are a favorite find. These are small repositories of someone's history, where thread ends were carefully wrapped around little pieces of a map

or a letter and buttons were sewn on squares cut from packaging. Though the thread is weakened with age and no longer good for sewing, Susan uses it as a linear element, embedding it in modeling compound or wrapping it around wood and adhering it with medium. Susan uses this technique in *Sewing Sisters* (page 84) to refer back to the act of sewing and to the woman who kept the thread basket. Her torso is a cotton Knit-Cro-Sheen ball. She offers us thread and carries another sewing sister on the back of her hat. So we are connected by the act of stitching across the generations.

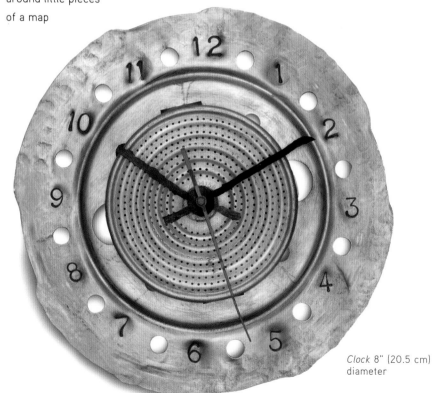

Clock 8" (20.5 cm) diameter

USES FOR ART SUPPLY WASTE

We find waste art materials another source of great inspiration. Things used in the studio, whether a dried-up paint tube, a palette, or a paintbrush painted down to a nubbin, have a kind of energy that resonates with the vigor of past use. *The Secret of Happiness/Paint Tube Babies* (page 85) is an ongoing series that delights in the materials we love to use.

It pays to make friends with local businesses. We get wonderful paper and aluminum offset plates from our local printer. Sometimes a business will put aside scraps we are particularly seeking. Sometimes we buy them for the recycler's price. Most of the time businesses know they are throwing out a lot of perfectly viable materials and appreciate our wanting to use them.

STOP! LOOK! LISTEN!

We could go on and on. For now, we urge you to honor attics and outbuildings and collections both random and methodical. Believe in critical mass. To a mixed-media object maker, everything has potential for reuse. Green studio practices not only help to save the planet, they also save money and time. So, start paying attention now. ✴

Overland 9½" × 9"
(24 × 23 cm)

Little Librarian
3¾" (9.5 cm) figure on
2" × 4" (5 10 cm) chair;
arm span is 7" (18 cm).

Shell Seekers/Tide Zones
1¾" (4.5 cm) square
carved wood scraps
vary in height from
4½" to 6½".

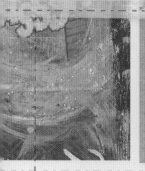

the MIXED ADVENTURES of a SUPERHERO series

by june pfaff daley

Call as Needed 12" × 12" (30.5 × 30.5 cm)

Since Superman's debut back in 1938, countless superheroes have been created and written into comic books, many crossing over into television and film. At first glance, one is drawn to their physical appearance. Beneath this, however, is the more lasting moral vision they suggest to us. I've come to realize that there is a superhero inside each of us. We might not wear a spandex costume or be able to leap tall buildings in a single bound, but in our own unique ways, we have the power to mold and change lives. At the same time, the modern-day superwoman is faced with unrealistic expectations regarding home, career, relationships, and physical appearance.

In this mixed-media series, connected primarily by color and concept, I celebrate the superhero inside every woman. I zeroed in on a palette that consists primarily of four colors (not including white and black), and I added a variety of remnant fabrics, vintage trims, papers, beads, and even old cookie-press parts.

The Power of Accessories 12" × 12" (30.5 × 30.5 cm)

materials

- ☐ Stretched canvas or other substrate of choice
- ☐ Sketching supplies
- ☐ A container for gathering papers and embellishments
- ☐ A variety of papers (book and magazine pages, decorative papers, etc.)
- ☐ Acrylic paints (I used dioxazine purple, ultramarine blue, quinacridone gold, and robin egg blue.)
- ☐ Paintbrushes
- ☐ Rags for wiping paints
- ☐ Matte medium
- ☐ Various utensils (for applying matte medium)
- ☐ Tim Holtz Distress Inks
- ☐ Gelly Roll pens (for tiny details)
- ☐ Clear satin varnish
- ☐ Embellishments of choice (I added beads, string, letters, bits of doilies and felt, and glitter.)

optional
- ☐ Scissors

often invisible

Opposite: *I Wear My Cape* 16" × 12"
(40.5 × 30.5 cm)

Above: *Often Invisible* 10" × 10"
(25.5 × 25.5 cm)

DIRECTIONS

1 Begin with rough sketches and
   text to feature on each piece.

2 Refine your sketches and develop
   the layout.

3 Start an idea box (an empty plastic
   container or a cardboard box)
   and fill it with any papers and

embellishments from your stash
that even remotely relate to the
piece(s) you have in mind. For
example, with *I Wear My Cape*,
I pulled old cookbooks, paper
doilies, and pieces of trim that
might be part of an apron. Ads
that related to women from a
1930s magazine also went into the

box. I added metal scrapbooking letters spelling hero, a space-themed wallpaper scrap, and old comic books.

---

tip: I never end up using every item in my idea box for a piece, but the exercise helps me zero in on suitable elements without being overwhelmed.

4   Re-create the layout from your sketches by cutting or tearing papers to size. Using matte medium, adhere the papers as the first layer. Allow to dry.

---

tip: I rely on matte medium to create texture by applying it with various utensils, including my fingers.

5   Add paint, avoiding heavy application in areas that you want to remain translucent so the papers beneath will show through. Remove or add paint by dragging a rag across the canvas. I used quinacridone gold to create the glowing edges around the woman's apron and to cast an intriguing glow in the other works.

6   Go back in and attach more collage elements. I used paint to incorporate the additions into the compositions. In some cases, I added glitter, as in *Call as Needed* (page 90).

7   Add handwritten phrases as desired.

8   When the majority of brush painting is complete, including the handwritten phrases, add paint drips. I watered down robin egg blue and let it run from the top,

down the canvas. I also spattered paint by flicking my brush over certain areas.

9   Attach any details that you want to keep relatively paint free, like the ruffle on the apron, the bead on the friend's tiara, and the lasso accessory.

10 Add final details. I used Tim Holtz inks for aging and depth and a white Gelly Roll pen for tiny details.

11 To finish, seal the painting(s) with a clear satin varnish.

Taking on a series provided an opportunity to speak to more than one idea relating to women and superheroes. While I believe a series should go together, that doesn't mean the pieces need to have *everything* in common such as size, format, color, concept, and material. Choosing limited commonalities (in my case, concept and palette) will bind a series together. Like family, there are similarities, but the differences are what create excitement. That—plus a golden lasso and a tiara. ✴

Alteration Booth 13" × 7" × 4¼" (33 × 18 × 11 cm)

note: I started with housing for an old clock. After removing the clock, I coated the entire box with matte medium and attached tissue paper along with a doily to add unique texture. I nailed a wooden star to the circular opening where the clock face had been and attached an old thread spool to the box top with Liquid Nails. Inside the box, I added rusted hangers for the mask and cape, along with a mirror edged with paint. The cape and mask were handstitched from bits of doilies and felt, and then aged with coffee. After the box was assembled to my liking, I painted, added collage elements (similar to the 2-D pieces), and completed the box with sealer.

CUPCAKE CONCOCTIONS

by sue pelletier

Cupcakes make me smile. Cupcakes look impressive in a group, but perhaps more importantly, a cupcake will look fabulous standing alone. Cupcakes evoke thoughts of a happy and simple childhood and fond memories of celebrations. Sprinkles, sugar, piping, and special candies all add personality to these individual pieces of heaven. Do I dare admit, another thing I love about cupcakes is you don't have to share! A cupcake is all yours—eat it slowly, save it for later, eat it quickly, or savor it with a glass of cold milk . . . it's up to you. It's your special treat.

DIRECTIONS
make the cupcakes

1   Choose a base for your cupcake sculptures. The pastel ramekins I selected seemed perfect because they were fluted, giving the dish that cupcake-paper look. Vintage metal baking tins would be fun to use.

2   Embellish the base. I used cloth measuring tape because I love the way the vintage numbers ground the piece. You could also use ribbon, lace, or bric-a-brac. Use a heavy matte gel medium to attach the measuring tape.

3   Stuff the base with tissue paper, filling it to the approximate height and width you want the cake to be. This becomes your armature.

4   Roll out a piece of air-drying clay so that it's round and thick like a large pancake. Gently place this round piece on the tissue paper mound, being sure to have it touching the top edge of your base, thus forming the "cupcake."

5   Wet your fingers and gently play with the clay, smoothing and pinching until you are happy with the basic shape. Don't try to make it perfect; every cupcake has its own unique personality.

6   Tear up small pieces of colored tissue paper and use matte gel medium to layer the tissue paper over the damp clay to create the frosting. Make sure you do this all in one sitting, because it's important that the clay is kept damp for the next step.

embellish the cupcakes

- - - - - - - - - - - - - - - - - -

tip: I created my cupcakes on a lazy Susan so I could continually spin and rotate each piece. Because they are sculptural, you want to make sure you are covering all sides.

1   Begin with the largest embellishment. In my case, it was a Tinkertoy top. Brush gel medium onto the bottom of the embellishment and gently press it onto the top of the cupcake. The gel medium helps it to adhere, but also, as the clay dries it shrinks a bit, making the embellishment fit snugly in the clay.

2   Attach the other embellishments in the same way, adding a dollop of gel medium and applying gentle pressure as you stick them into the damp clay.

materials

- [ ] An interesting base for your cupcake (I used pastel ramekins from a discount store.)
- [ ] Self-hardening clay
- [ ] Colored tissue paper
- [ ] Embellishments for the cupcake and the cupcake base
- [ ] Pins for attaching pieces to dangle
- [ ] Tinkertoys or other small toys
- [ ] Gel medium
- [ ] Spray glitter
- [ ] Walnut stain spray

ideas for embellishment

➡ I added some Artgirlz felt beads (which I thought added the perfect dash of whimsy) and some dangly pieces such as lockets, keys, and charms.

➡ I used some fun stick pins that I just stuck into the clay. I liked the way that looked, so I added some height by sticking the pins in just a bit. Funky brads were also pressed into the clay.

➡ To build up my Tinkertoy top, I added a stick through the top and into the clay to make a little flagpole for my celebration message. I added game pieces and odds and ends to the wood base for height and interest.

➡ The flag message at the top was created separately using an old schoolbook, letter stickers, etc. This message was added to the stick using gel medium and topped with a pin or doodad.

finishing

Give your cupcakes a final flourish. Depending on the look you want to achieve, you can age them with walnut spray stain, give them pizzazz with spray glitter, or add a bit of black carbon pencil along the edge for depth and texture. ✳

EXTRA

50 PAPERS ➡ FOR COLLAGE

1	Book pages	26	Newspaper
2	Candy wrappers	27	Old drawings and paintings
3	Catalog and magazine pages	28	Old notes and letters
4	Cocoon strippings	29	Origami papers
5	Coffee filters (used and unused)	30	Pamphlets
6	Confetti	31	Pattern tissue
7	Decorative papers	32	Photocopies
8	Directions	33	Player-piano paper
9	Doilies	34	Rag paper
10	Envelopes	35	Receipts
11	Foreign language papers	36	Recipes
12	Fortunes	37	Rice paper
13	Gift wrap	38	Sandpaper
14	Grid paper	39	Scrapbook papers
15	Grocery bags	40	Sheet music
16	Handmade paper	41	Shopping lists
17	Kraft paper	42	Stamps
18	Labels	43	Stickers
19	Lace paper	44	Teabag paper
20	Ledger pages	45	Tickets
21	Lotka paper	46	Tissue paper
22	Manila tags	47	Transfers
23	Maps	48	Vellum
24	Mulberry paper	49	Vintage photos
25	Napkins	50	Wallpaper

25 found objects ➡ FOR ASSEMBLAGE or MARK MAKING

1. Blocks
2. Bottle caps
3. Branches
4. Buttons
5. Cigar boxes
6. Combs
7. Corks
8. Doll clothes and shoes
9. Doll parts and furniture
10. Empty spools
11. Eating and cooking utensils
12. Faux food
13. Flower frogs
14. Game pieces
15. Jewelry boxes
16. Jewelry parts
17. Keys
18. Miniature bottles
19. Small toys
20. Snow fencing and chicken wire
21. Stirrers/straws
22. Tubing
23. Washers, screws, nails, etc.
24. Watch parts
25. Wires

ALL TORN UP
An Approach to Collage

by elizabeth st. hilaire nelson

Lemon Dream 12" × 12" (30.5 × 30.5 cm)

I can't tell you how many times I am asked by people admiring my collage work: "You really don't paint on top?" It's okay to ask: after all, it's hard to believe that the entire image is created from torn bits of paper and not brushstrokes of paint.

To create a collage, I start with a compositional sketch, followed by a loose acrylic underpainting on a wood panel. This underpainting becomes completely obscured by multiple bits of torn handmade, handpainted, and found papers that are adhered over the top.

The torn paper technique ultimately becomes the primary focus of my figurative collage work. I collect art paper and I am always on the lookout for collage material. I expand my color choices by hand stamping, decorating, and monoprinting my own papers and book pages to add to my collection. Collage allows me to respond to the materials and imagery, so that the art can evolve from the give and take, the push and pull of colors and textures.

tip: The level of difficulty for this project is moderate; collage can be a very forgiving medium. If you don't like the way a piece looks and you work fast enough, you can pull off that piece of paper. If you decide later that you still don't like it, you can just cover it with another piece of paper. However, as with any other artistic process, collage requires the same understanding of the elements of design: space, shape, line, value, color, texture and pattern, and composition.

materials

- [ ] Wood panel such as hardboard, luann, or ¼" (6 mm) plywood
- [ ] Liquitex Acrylic Gloss Gel Medium (for use as glue)
- [ ] Filbert synthetic brushes, medium size
- [ ] Semigloss acrylic varnish (I use Golden UV brand.)
- [ ] A small pot of water to keep your glue brush moist and clean
- [ ] A variety of papers: handmade, painted, old book pages, found papers, wallpaper, maps, etc.

Pencil sketch on wood panel.

The underpainting: simplify the details and establish the values.

Establish dark areas to recede (the background trees) and the light areas to advance (the sidewalk and the flower bed in the foreground).

Process photos by Elizabeth St. Hilaire Nelson.

For Two 12" × 12" (30.5 × 30.5 cm)

DIRECTIONS
where to start

I work from photos. My husband is an artist and a photographer, and he provides me with wonderful reference images. My high school art teacher provides me with a totally different style of photos. And then there are the photos I have collected over the years and those I have taken myself. I crop and combine my reference photos using Photoshop software until I have just the right image in just the right proportions. I use the photo as a reference and a starting point. My finished collage is much richer in texture and color than the original photo. I love color and patterns, so I push the image to be something much more expressive than simply a copy of a photo.

Two Blue 12" × 12" (30.5 × 30.5 cm)

the base

1 Establish a sketch based on your photo, but simplify it. This collage technique usually works best with large and clearly defined subject matter without tons of tiny details.

Keep this in mind when you are sketching and simplify the details to something you can work with.

2 To create your underpainting, cover the whole board with acrylic paint; it will act as a primer. If you want to prime the wood first

and then paint, that works, too. I use the underpainting as a way to block in the color and values of my subject matter. I also rely on it to provide some color in the space between strips of paper that might not come together perfectly, kind of like the way a pastel artist will work on colored paper rather than pure white.

tip: I can't stress this part enough: don't fall in love with your underpainting and go crazy making it look like a finished piece of art. You are going to cover it up anyway, so just make it quick and simple.

tip: It does not matter if your wood surface is perfectly smooth; you will be covering it with paper.

tear it up

Now that your base is painted, begin layering your collage papers.

1 Choose the area of the collage you want to work on first and gather your collage papers together, selecting the colors and hues you will need. Some of my favorite sources of collage materials are handmade paper by local artists, old books from used-book stores, and my children's schoolwork papers.

2 As you work, coat both sides of your collage papers with the gloss gel medium. I achieve this by painting the "glue" on top of the underpainting in the area I plan to work on (only paint small areas at one time as this glue dries fast), laying the paper into the glue, and then brushing another layer of glue over the paper to seal it. By doing this, you are sealing the papers from the air and, in effect, making them archival.

3 Continue to layer collage papers over one another until you have achieved the look you want. To create the painterly effect of my collage work, I collage multiple layers of papers. I rarely lay down one layer of paper and move on; the weaving of different textures and colors is what makes the effect most unique and interesting.

finishing touches

1 Let the collage dry overnight to be sure all the layers of glue are dry and come back to it in the morning with a fresh set of eyes. You may find an area you overlooked that still needs work, or you may look at your piece and say "Wow! That looks really great." If you are experiencing the "wow" feeling, you are ready to apply the varnish coat.

2 Brush on two coats of varnish following the directions on the product. I use a Golden product. Liquitex also makes a good-quality UV varnish.

tips

➡ Be careful not to overwork the varnish when brushing it on, as that can give it a fogged or cloudy appearance.

➡ Brush very slowly and evenly so as not to stir up bubbles in the varnish by introducing air into it.

➡ Look at the freshly varnished piece at an angle, in good light, to be sure you haven't missed any spots.

➡ Collage should be fun. Enjoy incorporating interesting and meaningful papers in your work. This gives the viewer a reason to linger and look more closely at your collage. ✳

design tips for your collage

Keep in mind the importance of establishing light and shadow; this is what defines form and figure. You can use any color of the rainbow and any pattern of paper to create your subject, but what is most important is establishing the color values.

Use multiple layers of papers overlapped with new colors and values in order to make the imagery work. As you can see, I don't limit myself to basic colors in my bits of paper; instead I use many colors to create an area of overall color.

Top: *Flavors of Fall* 18" × 24" (45.5 × 61 cm)

Bottom: *Florida Sunshine* 24" × 24" (61 × 61 cm)

Photos this page by Doug Nelson.

CHARACTER STUDY
text as a collage element

by **lisa occhipinti**

on the second morning her beautiful French hour looked rather charming

Second Morning 6" × 6" (15 × 15 cm)

Letterforms, text, and writing have always been an obsession of mine. I have been including text as a collage element in my mixed-media paintings for years, and I often write on my canvases. One day I reached a fork in the road and thought: what if I allowed the letters themselves to take a greater role in the composition? I wanted the letters to be larger and more prominent. The paintings would be about the bowl of a lowercase "b" or about the looping descender of a "y." Thus began my series of mixed-media paintings I call *Character Studies*.

Above left: The surface is divided into thirds, and a wash has been applied.

Above right: Glazes have been applied to better define the three sections and paper collage added, in this case an old sewing pattern. The letterforms have been placed in the desired design with some of their shapes cropped.

materials

- ☐ Stretched or unstretched primed canvas, any size
- ☐ Acrylic paints (I use tubes of heavy-body acrylics by Golden Artist Colors.)
- ☐ Matte medium
- ☐ Flat paintbrushes
- ☐ Pencil
- ☐ Cups for water and paint
- ☐ Palette for mixing paint
- ☐ Palette knife
- ☐ X-Acto knife and a cutting mat
- ☐ Scissors
- ☐ Collage papers or other design materials

optional

- ☐ Computer and printer with Photoshop or another design program

DIRECTIONS

prepare the canvas

1 Divide the surface of your canvas into uneven thirds. Simply draw three light pencil lines horizontally, vertically, diagonally, or in a combination. It is sometimes difficult to begin when you're looking at a blank surface, and this is a good way to start.

2 Water down some paint and apply a tint to the canvas with a wash of color. Because washes are thin and light in hue, they are a great way to initiate color.

tip: I think it is best to start with a warm earthy tone, such as yellow ocher or raw sienna, for example, since whatever you put on top will become richer. Keep in mind that, even if you don't like this initial color wash, it will change and evolve as you continue to layer and work.

create the letterforms

I always choose letters for their shape and design without a concern for spelling out a word. If you have a specific word in mind, you can use those letters.

1 Create your text while the color wash is drying. You can do so in one of three ways:

→ Use Photoshop or another design program. I work with one letter per page so that I have room to transform it. Play around with the fonts in your library, being aware of their characteristics: serif, sans serif, bold, italic, gothic, script, etc. (see Letterform Mini Primer on page 109). Think about the feel you want to create in your painting and choose combinations of letters to suit that feeling. Graphic and linear. Curvy and elegant.

→ Use any word-processing software to size your letters, but note that you will have less control over the manipulation of your letters.

→ Write your letters by hand and manipulate the size and color as desired.

2 Consider the scale of your letters. I like large letters that accentuate their details. I also like to crop them to make their form more dynamic. You can print a letter as large as your printer paper.

- -

tip: If you're using a design program, change the letter so that it is only the outline of the letter. If you're using word-processing software, you can change your text color to white letters, and the highlight color to black. Please respect the font designer's work and check the copyright permissions.

3 Apply color to your letterforms. Paint the letters with your acrylics, opaquely or with a glaze. Don't worry about staying in the lines. Once they are fully dry, carefully cut out the letters and set them aside.

- -

tip: I use an X-Acto knife since it is more precise, especially if you have little curlicue areas, but you can also use scissors.

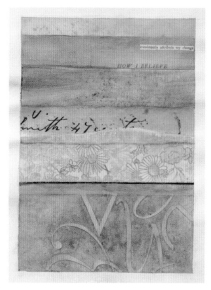

Believe 9" × 12" (23 × 30.5 cm)

Summer Flourish 9" × 12" (23 × 30.5 cm)

Stepping Stones 6" × 6" (15 × 15 cm)

washes and glazes

There are many ways to apply paint besides using it right out of the tube. Washes and glazes are my mainstays for paint application. Both of them are a means of lightening up the saturation of the paint hue, yet they are very different in nature. I work in this method so I can control the colors and values of the painting slowly and thoughtfully. It is difficult to get too dark or too heavy with color when you are working in transparent layers.

A wash is when you add water to the paint. This not only dilutes the color, but it breaks down the body of the paint so it is a watery liquid. I like to pour and drip the watery paint onto the surface to create organic visual texture. Washes are delicate, transparent, and movable like watercolor.

A glaze is made by adding matte medium to the paint color. Like a wash, the color will lighten, but the body of the paint remains viscous. It will not drip or pool, but rather glide onto the surface. You can also use gloss medium, which will dry with a glossy finish. ✳

LETTERFORM ➡ MINI PRIMER

a a *a* **a** b g

serif   sans serif   italic   bold

ascender

descender

An example of the different letter shapes as they would appear outlined in a design program. Consider choosing letters for their form or use them to spell out a specific word.

CHAPTER **5**

MIXED-MEDIA
stitching

Stitching is not just something you find embellishing fabric creations—not anymore. Handstitching, embroidery stitches, and even free-motion machine stitching grace both fabric and paper. Sometimes stitches create simple attachments; other times they bring the piece to life. In this chapter, artists show how hand and machine stitching can add color and dimension to your collages and bookmaking.

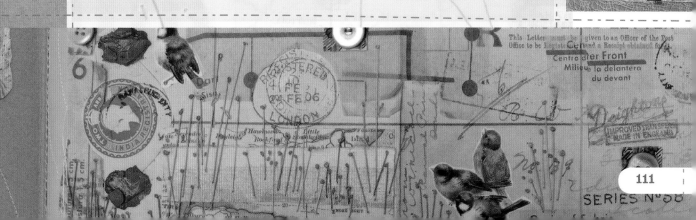

PAPER COLLAGE QUILTS

by annette morgan

Green Ice 12½" × 12½" (31.5 × 31.5 cm)

Much of my designing is paper-based, and many of my quilts and textile designs are built on my addiction to collage. My workbooks and notebooks are full of collage designs, some very simple and others more complicated. It must stem from my love of all types of paper: bought papers, handmade papers, homemade paper, and hand-decorated papers. One of my favorite shops is Paperchase in London's Tottenham Court Road. It has racks and racks of different papers from all parts of the world. One of my favorite books on collage is by Gerald Brommer, called *Collage Techniques: A Guide for Artists and Illustrators* (Watson-Guptill, 1994). It has amazing images from many different artists and several sections with how-to techniques.

materials

- ☐ Heavy, good-quality paper, such as drawing paper
- ☐ A variety of paintbrushes
- ☐ Favorite printing stamps
- ☐ A selection of acrylic paint
- ☐ Inks (whatever you have, including leftover Procion dye)
- ☐ A rigid plastic sheet
- ☐ Roller (brayer)
- ☐ Colored tissue paper
- ☐ Acrylic gloss medium

I enjoy playing with collage, combining my love of dyed fabrics, handstitching threads, and paper. I could spend hours playing and designing. On this journey, which you can travel with me here, I describe how to decorate paper, dye sticks, and assemble them with fabric into different collage designs.

DECORATING PAPERS

paper 1
painting and printing

1. Lay a sheet of the heavy paper on your work surface and paint it with diluted inks.

2. Let the paper dry and then stamp it with a favorite stamp that has been brushed with acrylic paint.

tip: I often put two different colors of paint into a tray and make sure there is a little of each on my brush; this gives a nice effect on the stamp.

paper 2
monoprinting

1. Put a blob of acrylic paint onto the rigid plastic sheet and spread it around with a brush.

2. Using the stick end of the brush, draw patterns into the paint. Grouting tools work well, too.

3. Press a sheet of the heavy paper onto the surface of the plastic and pull it away. The designs will now be on the paper. There will still be some color left on the plastic sheet, and you can get another image if you moisten it with a little water.

4. Leave the paper to dry and then paint additional designs with inks or Procion dye.

paper 3
rolling

1. Put a blob of acrylic paint onto the rigid plastic and roll through it with your roller until it is loaded with paint.

2. Roll the paint onto the heavy paper. You can use the whole roller to put color onto your paper or use the roller to make marks across the paper by pressing the roller onto the paper instead of rolling it.

tip: I often put inks onto the plastic, too, and use the roller; this gives a softer effect than just paint.

paper 4
colored tissue paper

1. Place scrunched-up colored tissue paper on a sheet of heavy paper that has been painted with water.

2. Leave the tissue in place until dry; then remove the tissue and you will have a sheet of paper with delicate colored marks.

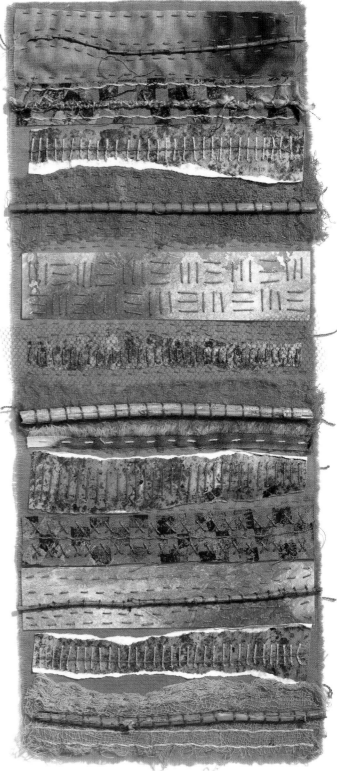

3 Decorate this paper using any of the painting, printing, and rolling techniques described above.

tips

→ Play around with these ideas until you have a pile of papers.

→ When dry, paint the papers with acrylic medium; this gives a good finish, a tip gleaned from Ruth Issett.

→ Try mixing an iridescent medium with the acrylic paint to get a slight sparkly effect.

DYED STICKS

You can collect dried sticks from your garden or hedge, or you can use wooden barbeque sticks, the type used for kebabs.

directions

1 Cut the sticks to a manageable size; I usually cut the barbeque sticks in half to about 5½" (14 cm).

2 Lay them in a deep tray and pour some Procion dye (cold-water dye) over them; you don't have to add anything else to the dye.

3 Leave for several hours and then drain the excess fluid away. No need to rinse the sticks.

4 Leave to dry overnight. If they are not quite dry the next morning, just shake them about and leave for a few more hours.

tip: If the sticks are left to dry on paper towels, the paper will absorb the dye and the papers can then be used in collage.

MAKING A LONG PANEL

1 Tear a strip of fabric into a rectangle about 5½" x 13" (14 × 33 cm). I like to tear my fabrics and papers; this gives an interesting edge that you don't have to neaten.

2 Cut or tear narrow strips of fabric and paper.

3 Place your fabric rectangle in front of you and start to place your fabric and paper strips onto the base fabric.

4 Next, place the wooden sticks onto the fabric and paper.

5 When you are happy with the placement, lightly apply the glue in little dots and secure all the strips and sticks in place. Leave to dry for about an hour before you stitch.

6 If your fabric is very lightweight, place it on another layer of fabric to prevent puckering when you handstitch.

7 Start to stitch. I use very simple stitches such as a running stitch, whipped running stitch (running stitch done first and then another thread used just on the top, woven in and out of the running stitch), cross-stitch, seed stitch, and long stitch.

8 Secure the sticks with a couching stitch; this just means a vertical stitch to hold it in place.

tip: Mount your finished piece onto a different colored cardstock and frame it.

materials

- ☐ Hand-dyed fabrics in several strong colors
- ☐ Dyed sticks
- ☐ A sheet of one of the papers decorated as above
- ☐ Scraps of open-weave fabrics, such as colored net or scrim
- ☐ Handsewing thread and needle
- ☐ White glue, such as Tacky Glue (This has a fine nozzle tip that will come in handy, or you can use a cocktail stick.)

MAKING A LARGER COLLAGE

1 Tear your background fabric into two large squares; I used 12½" (31.5 cm) squares.

2 Lay one fabric square on your work surface, right side down, and cut a piece of batting to fit, just slightly smaller than the square.

3 Spray the fabric with a fabric adhesive, such as 505 spray, and lay the batting on the fabric. Spray the batting with the adhesive and lay the second square of fabric on top. This will hold the layers (your quilt sandwich) together without you having to pin or tack.

4 Tear the remaining fabric and paper into strips and arrange them into a pleasing design. ✷

MIX AND STITCH

by dorit elisha

My sewing machine has been my favorite art tool for the last ten years or so. It is always standing on my worktable, ready to go. I use it on most of my artwork, whether it's made of fabric or paper. Many times sewing replaces the use of glue, since I attach the layered papers or fabrics by stitching them to the background. Sometimes, as a means of drawing or painting, I create lines and shapes just by stitching. I also like the texture that the stitching adds to the artwork.

I grew up with my mother and grandmother sewing constantly. Buying new clothes wasn't always affordable, so they sewed dresses for themselves and for the girls in the family, many times recycling old dresses or big shirts. I once made my living by sewing and selling my designed clothing. Later, when I became more involved with art, it was a natural step for me to connect stitching with art.

Printmaking is another important part of my art. I make prints usually without using a printing press, and very often I combine my prints, or parts of them, in my mixed-media stitched art.

The process of my creation is very intuitive and spontaneous. I start with a general idea that may have been inspired by a piece of fabric or an image I saw or a color combination that looked appealing to me.

I select a piece of paper or fabric that will serve as a base, foundation, or substrate. Oftentimes I use an existing, unfinished artwork, like a monoprint I did in the past that didn't feel like a finished piece. It serves as a great colorful and textured background. I also tend to add sections of prints I have lying around my studio into this mix. These were made using different printmaking techniques (like collagraph

materials

☐ A foundation: This could be a blank piece of heavy paper such as Strathmore 65-lb. or a piece of upholstery fabric in a comfortable size for you. It could also be a collage or a print that you have started and didn't quite know how to finish.

☐ A focal point piece of fabric or paper with an image

☐ Several smaller pieces of fabric, paper, and fibers in colors that will complement the main image

☐ Sewing machine and thread

Cacti and Succulents 8" x 8" (20.5 x 20.5 cm). Detail opposite.
Cacti photos by Stephen Bay of Bay Images.

and screen printing). I treat my fabric and paper the same way when collage stitching and often mix the two in one artwork.

Here's how to create your own stitched collage.

DIRECTIONS

1   Sketch a draft of your desired composition.

2   Place the focal piece on the foundation and start adding the smaller pieces around it, moving them from one place to another until you are satisfied with your composition.

3   Pin the pieces down or use a touch of a glue stick to keep them in place while you start stitching. If you have a free-motion stitching foot for your machine, it will make the stitching easier.

4   Start by stitching the focal piece into place, then move to the surrounding pieces with or without lifting the needle. You can vary the look of the stitch by going from a regular running stitch to a zigzag in different widths. You can also alternate the color of the thread you are using.

5   When all the pieces are stitched into place you may add some more lines in other parts of your collage to emphasize or add texture to certain areas.

6   For a clean and finished look on the back side, add one more backing piece of fabric

or paper by stitching it only to the surrounding edges of the artwork.

tips

➡ If you want to add a page to an existing book (such as an altered book) by sewing the piece separately, glue it into the book as the last step, so it still looks like it was stitched directly into the book.

➡ Stitching on a large paper is easy if the paper is soft and bendable. You can roll it under the machine's arm, just like you would a large quilt.

➡ Keep your needles for stitching paper separate from those for fabric sewing.

➡ Combining paper and fabric in the same artwork adds some very interesting texture. ✹

Opposite: The focal point of this stitched collage (12¾" x 17½" [32 x 44.5 cm]) is a screen print of a vintage photo.

SEALED WITH A STITCH

by **viv sliwka**

The decorative quality of vintage ephemera has always had a great appeal to me and nothing more so than vintage envelopes and letters. The muted, worn colors and textures of these items, whether from home or abroad, with text both mechanically stamped and handwritten, provide an interesting backdrop on which to combine collage and embroidery, breathing new life into a transient item.

materials

☐ Paper ephemera

☐ Scraps of fabric, laces, and trims

☐ Glue stick

☐ Favorite embroidery threads

☐ Embroidery needles

☐ Buttons

I enjoy using found papers in my work and prefer vintage envelopes for the stories they can tell. I think to myself, "Who was it who wrote with such a fine hand?" "Did he survive the war?" "Why did she write that letter?" All of these unanswered questions are part of the joy of working with these little snippets of everyday history. But I would also consider using a special, maybe newer, envelope—one that contains good news, for example. If the envelope has an interesting date on the back, I open the envelope up, so that all the points of interest can be seen.

PREPARATION

Sorting through my stash of found papers and ephemera is part of my process. Thumbing through old books and magazines until I find the right imagery and text is also a big part. (Be aware of copyright when doing this.) For example, the sweet little girl that I used—it just felt right to use her, instinct you may say—has nothing whatsoever to do with the envelope itself. It is all part of expressing one's particular interests.

What I have in mind as I work is to build a coherent visual piece using collected papers and fabrics from many sources. I sometimes include my own drawings or monoprints. I want to achieve depths of opacity, with added text, color, and texture. I use embroidery to highlight not only my love of flowers, but also my love of the decorative stitch. With embroidery, I bring surface texture, color, and interest to my work; I take each piece down another avenue and have more fun with it.

The final touch is the addition of buttons: wonderful, beautiful, old buttons. They, too, have a story to tell, even better if they are from your mother's or grandmother's button box! I adore how they catch the light or brighten a piece of work with their cheery colors, shapes, and sizes; somehow they just finish the piece beautifully. I could work these pieces all day, every day.

DIRECTIONS
mail art

1   Select an envelope. You may want to use one that holds sentimental value or a found envelope with beautiful stamps and text.

2   Using a glue stick, apply found papers and scraps of fabric, lace,

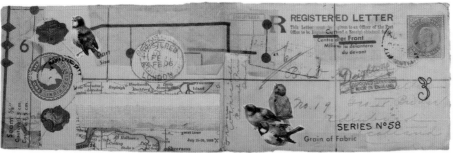

Above, top: A vintage envelope cut along three sides and opened so that both the front and back are visible.

Above, center: Paper ephemera is glued to the envelope

Above, bottom: Additional embellishments, such as hand embroidery and buttons, complete the design.

and trims. Use pieces of maps, sewing patterns, and textured handmade papers, hiding and highlighting areas to please visually.

3 Start stitching. Let your needle do the talking.

4 Finish with vintage buttons.

needle case

I particularly enjoy making needle cases. In this instance, I took an old envelope that had lots of interest, including beautiful stamps and a date mark. I collaged the envelope with paper ephemera (i.e., a map, sewing pattern paper, and even the backing paper from an old hook-and-eye package). When I was happy with the collaging, I copied the piece onto ink-jet transfer paper and ironed the transfer onto fabric. I then added beautiful snippets of fabric and embroidery for surface texture.

To make the needle case, I sandwiched interfacing between the covers (fused and machine-stitched along all four edges). The pages of the needle case are hand-dyed felt (cut with pinking shears). I finished off the case with favorite mother-of-pearl and vintage buttons. ✴

EXTRA

➡ FOUR EASY HANDSTITCHES

Handstitching is a wonderful way to embellish your artwork, adding texture and interest. Whether you're working on fabric, paper, or even metal, stitches can really add that little something extra. You'll find many beautiful embroidery threads and other fibers to explore.

Backstitch

Backstitch is excellent for making lines, outlining shapes, adding details, and drawing forms with thread. The stitch is worked right to left, opposite to the usual direction of handstitching (**fig. 1**). The more consistent your stitches, the better the line will look.

French Knot

You can use French knots to make dots or stitch in multiples to make lines and other design shapes. To make a French knot, wrap thread around a needle once or twice, and then insert the needle in the fabric without losing the wrap, as shown in **fig. 2**. If the dot you create isn't as large as you'd like, use a thicker thread rather than more wraps of the thread.

Satin Stitch

Satin stitch, a series of flat stitches placed very close together, is a wonderful way to fill shapes. You can work satin stitches in any direction. It's important to keep the edges even and to cover any outline markings by taking the stitching to the outside of the outline (**fig. 3**).

Chain Stitch

Chain stitches resemble the links of a chain and are formed by stitching a series of connected loops (**fig. 4**). They are an easy surface embellishment that you can use to form lines and to draw shapes.

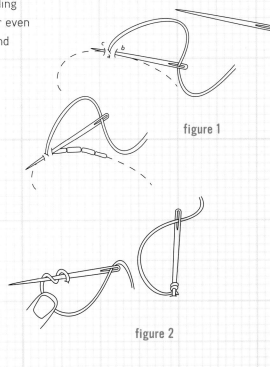

figure 1

figure 2

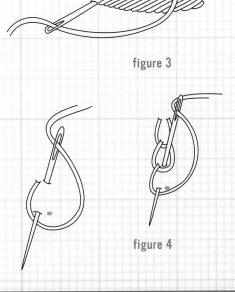

figure 3

figure 4

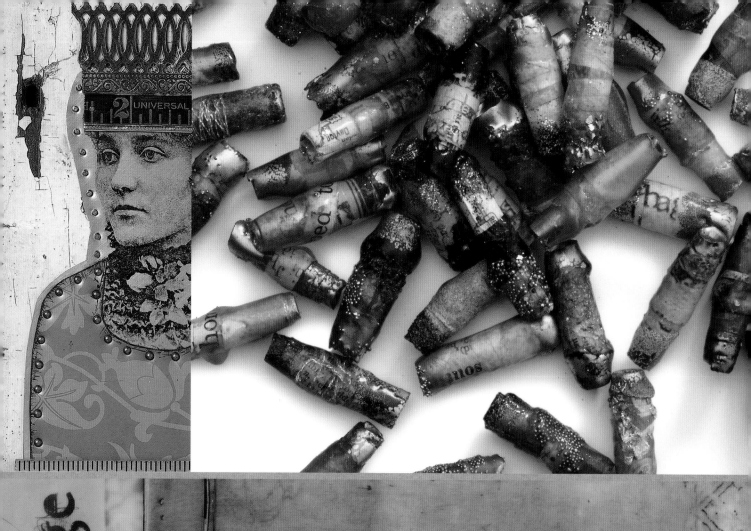

Eco-Fashion Comes of Age

The LOCAL

CHAPTER 6

MIXED MEDIA AND **BEYOND**
encaustic, metal, and jewelry

Still looking to add that little something extra to your artwork? Include some metal. You can paint it, stamp it, emboss it, and more. Or make some paper beads to string or to embellish a piece of art. Try some encaustic. In this chapter, artists share their expertise to demystify these popular mixed-media techniques.

the ENCAUSTIC COLLAGE

by patricia baldwin seggebruch

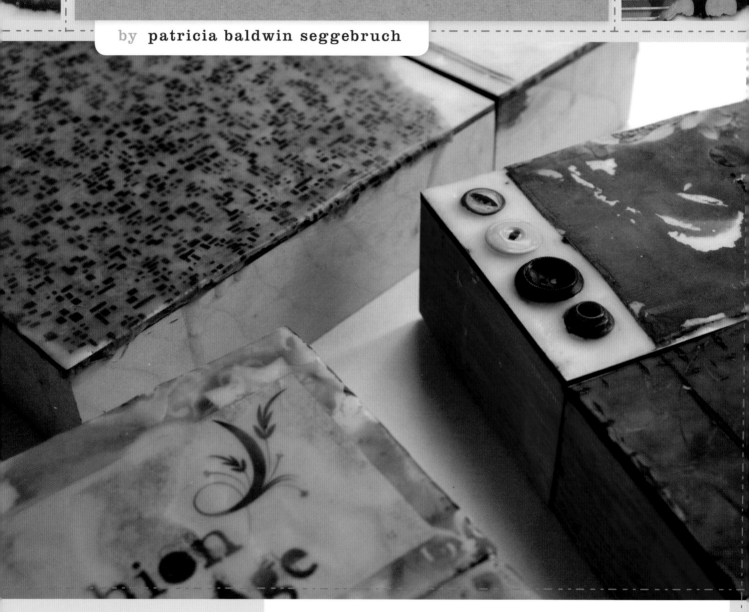

I don't journal. I didn't grow up with a floral, pink, plastic, locked diary, nor did I pen my thoughts in a collection of notebooks hidden under my mattress. It just wasn't part of my world. So imagine my surprise when about three years ago I began a series in wax that was very reminiscent of journalistic musings.

During these past three years I've come to not only thrive in the expression of emotions in wax journaling, but have taken up pen and paper to write pages of musings as well. The joy of self-expression in wax is like no other I have identified with. To be able to share it with an audience and see their connection to the emotions and images I have worked into the wax is a soul-opening, creative lifeboat that has propelled not only my artistic path, but my emotional expression and self-expression, too.

The techniques introduced here are varied and geared toward the encaustic artist who has at least delved into the basics of wax painting, if not become an expert.

DIRECTIONS

Each of my pieces consists of two Claybord surfaces, as called for in the materials list. I work back and forth between the two units to ensure a visually cohesive finished piece, and when the design is complete, I secure the pieces together permanently. When starting, I set out with a general idea of what I want to say in the wax and choose art papers to set this into motion. When I feel I've achieved a sense of what I intend to translate to the wax, I consider the texture and also decide whether to add words, letters, and/or numbers, and whether to scribe into the wax to make a statement.

1   Choose art papers that speak to the message you want to translate into the wax: colors, textures, and patterns that begin to tell your story. With the right base papers to begin your journaling—colors and patterns that play into what you plan to build in the wax—you establish a foundation on which to base the subsequent journaling story. For instance, in the piece below right, I chose to begin with vibrant green paper to suggest new growth and a fresh start. Cut or tear the papers as desired and then set them aside.

2   Apply the heat gun to the 8" × 8" (20.5 × 20.5 cm) Claybord until it is warm to the touch. Then spread a layer of wax medium over the entire surface to create a primed layer. Heat again with the gun in order to fuse this wax layer to the board (fig. 1).

tip: I put large amounts of wax into printmaker's tins and place them on my palette (griddle) to melt the wax. This way I have plenty of melted wax at the ready.

materials

- ☐ Encaustic palette or a griddle reserved for this purpose
- ☐ Hake brushes
- ☐ Printmaker's tins (seamless metal ink cans)
- ☐ Ampersand Claybord, smooth: 8" × 8" × 2" (20.5 × 20.5 × 5 cm) and 4" × 8" × 2" (10 × 20.5 × 5 cm)
- ☐ Encaustic medium
- ☐ Heat gun
- ☐ Assorted art papers
- ☐ Pigment sticks
- ☐ Awl
- ☐ Metal ruler

fig. 1

If you haven't had your life, what have you had?

IF YOU HAVEN'T HAD YOUR LIFE, WHAT HAVE YOU HAD?

IF IT FEELS GOOD, IT'S GUIDANCE

3 After the wax has cooled slightly, apply your precut art papers to select areas (fig. 2). After you have added the art paper, apply another layer of wax medium over it and fuse again with the heat gun to incorporate this added layer of paper and wax to the initial primed layer (fig. 3).

4 Work the 4" × 8" (10 × 20.5 cm) piece in the same manner as the larger piece, following Steps 2 and 3.

5 If you wish, add words, letters, or numbers to make a statement. To do so, just tear portions of text from papers and embed them in the layers as you did previously.

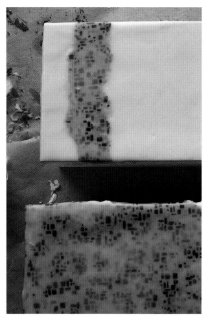

fig. 2

fig. 3

tip: I felt that the inclusion of burned glue-paper and handmade paper beads set the tone nicely. I simply added a bit of hot wax to the area where I wanted to place them and embedded them in layers in a manner similar to the previous collaging process. (Burned glue-paper is tissue paper or other that I've smeared with wood glue and then hit with a propane torch flame. The flame "cooks" the glue on the paper and burns it into the paper, creating a very cool new look. Always take extra caution when working with an open flame.)

6 If desired, scribe into the warm wax to create incised lines. In the example, I used an awl and a straight edge to create two parallel lines.

7 When you are satisfied with your scribing, allow the wax to cool to room temperature and then rub pigment stick into the incised lines and shapes.

tip: I like to rub pigment stick liberally over the entire surface, allowing any imperfections in the wax surface, as well as the incised lines, to catch the pigments (fig. 4). I then remove the excess with a paper towel.

8 To add an image transfer in the form of a phrase, type your phrase, print it in mirror image, and then make a copy. If the wax has cooled, warm it gently with the heat gun and place the copy facedown on the wax. Burnish the back of the copy paper to transfer the words to the waxed surface.

9 Dampen the paper with a few spritzes of water. This will relax the fibers and cause them to release the image to the wax. Burnish again, and then peel away the paper; the words will remain.

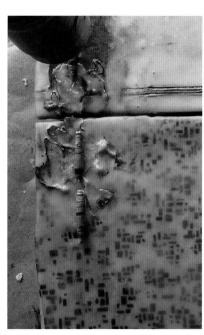

fig. 4

Sometimes life knows best

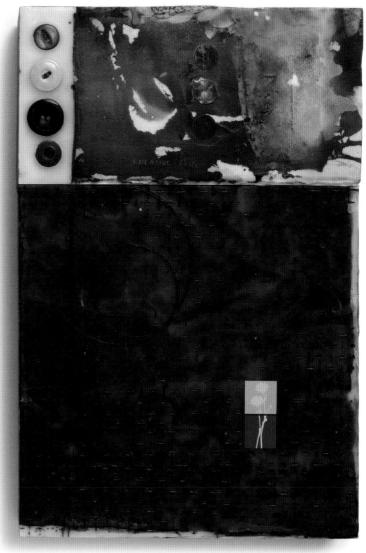

10 Reflect on what you've done to be sure it speaks cohesively. Did you successfully translate your message to the wax? If not, work with the surface until you are satisfied.

11 To finish, the boards can be fused together permanently with heavy-duty glue or screws, or left separate. ✳

EXTRA

→ MAKE IT STICK: A GUIDE TO ADHESIVES

The materials you want to attach and the length of time you want the bond to last will determine your choice of adhesive. Because glues are relatively inexpensive, it makes sense to try different brands in the different categories to see which type works best for your application. Following are some of the most popular adhesives for mixed-media art.

All-Purpose Glues

These types of adhesives work when you just want to stick something together; they are perfect for general use.

Craft and Tacky Glues

Go with tacky or quick-dry glue when you're not worried about washability, permanence, and durability. Try Crafter's Pick Incredibly Tacky or Aleene's Tacky brands.

Permanent Glues

When you're working with nonporous items such as glass, plastic, or metal, this is the glue to make them stick. Try Duncan's Liquid Fusion brand or Beacon Adhesives Quick Grip. Permanent glues offer a variety of special features; check the label if you want a glue that's weatherproof, flexible, or super strong.

Paper Adhesives

Because wrinkles and curling are a problem when gluing papers to each other or to other surfaces, it's important to choose the right glue:

Polyvinyl acetate (PVA): The bookbinder's standard, it is also used in framing, collage, and paper crafts. Try Lineco Neutral pH Adhesive or Crafter's Pick Memory Mount.

Glue sticks: Best used when gluing papers and other flat porous items. Burnishing often helps to make the components adhere. Try Scotch Craft Stick or UHU Stic brands.

Dimensional glue: This glue can be used in place of foam dots and mounting tapes to create a raised effect. Try Helmar Scrap Dots or Pop Up Glue Dots brands.

Fabric Adhesives

Some fabric glues dry quickly; some go on wet and must be fused with a dry iron. There are liquid, sticky, and iron-on varieties. Good fabric glue should be washable. Try Crafter's Pick Fabric Glue, Fabri-tac Permanent Fabric Adhesive, or Liquid Thread brands.

Gemstone and Jewelry Adhesives

These specialty glues are easy to use and can help when you want to add a little glitz to your mixed-media art and wearables. Try Beacon Adhesives Gem-Tac or Helmar Gemstone Glue brands.

METAL *magic*

by **beryl taylor**

Metal Magic 14¼" × 10½" (36 × 26.5 cm)

I've always enjoyed working with metal, and it took considerable time for me to find the perfect metal. Soft embossing copper is now my favorite; it's so soft and pliable, it's almost like working with fabric. At one time, I thought being able to emboss and stitch onto it would be the ultimate. But, with the amazing products now available, you can do so much more. Metal can even be distressed with gesso—wow! There are also a lot of products that can be used to add a patina to metal. You can apply heat and obtain amazing results, too, but I try to keep the process as safe as possible and am quite happy using paints and inks for coloring.

It always seemed to me, and to most people, that stitching metal with a sewing machine would be a no-no, but with this thin, soft metal it is no problem at all. I use a standard 90/14 needle and polyester thread (needle and bobbin) and do fine.

I cut a number of pieces of metal in lots of different sizes (1⅛" × 1⅜" [3 × 3.5 cm], ¾" × 5¼" [2 × 13.5 cm], 2¾" [7 cm] square, etc.) and decorated them with a variety of tools and techniques. I embossed and painted each piece and then added decorative details: distressing with gesso, more paint, some embellished metal elements, and ultra-thick embossing powders. When I was satisfied with my metal panels, I arranged them on a fabric/felt background and machine-stitched them in place. Finally, I added narrow raw-edge strips of fabric between the panels and secured the strips with embroidery stitches.

DIRECTIONS
metal background panels

1 Lay a large piece of metal, decorative face down, on a mouse pad. Place your chosen stencil on the metal and, using a ballpoint pen, draw around the design. When you have completed the drawing, take an embossing tool and go over the drawn lines to emphasize the image. You may wish to cut and emboss all of your background panels at one time. Be sure to save any metal scraps so you can add them as smaller decorative elements on the other panels; you can even emboss these, as well.

2 Paint the embossed metal panels with the glass paints, nail polish, or alcohol inks, and leave them to dry.

tip: The glass paints take longer to dry than the others.

materials

- [ ] Extra-soft embossing metal such as ArtEmboss
- [ ] Mouse pad, or similar
- [ ] Stencils
- [ ] Ballpoint pen
- [ ] Embossing tool
- [ ] Paintbrushes
- [ ] Coloring agents for metal, such as glass paints, alcohol-based inks, and nail polish
- [ ] Gesso
- [ ] Paper towels
- [ ] Modeling paste
- [ ] Glass bead gel
- [ ] Hole punch, regular and craft shapes (I use flowers and stars.)
- [ ] Watercolor paper
- [ ] Beads
- [ ] Strong glue such as E-6000
- [ ] Basic sewing supplies, including a needle for handstitching, scissors, and thread (When machine stitching metal, I use Gutermann 100% polyester thread.)
- [ ] Water-soluble paper
- [ ] Rubber stamps, deeply etched
- [ ] Acrylic paints
- [ ] Manufactured silk flowers
- [ ] Ultra-thick embossing powders
- [ ] Embossing stamp pad, clear
- [ ] Heat gun
- [ ] Sewing machine
- [ ] Decorative thread (I use DMC.)
- [ ] Unbleached cotton fabric
- [ ] Patterned cotton fabric
- [ ] Felt

3 Add decorative elements to the metal panels to create a variety of effects.

decorating the panels

These are the techniques I use for adding decorative elements to my embossed metal background panels. When your painted pieces are dry, use any combination of these ideas.

→ Paint your embossed panel(s) with gesso and then immediately wipe it off with a paper towel, leaving a small amount to give a distressed look.

→ Lay one of your stencils over part of an embossed metal background and spread modeling paste or glass bead gel over the stencil opening. Carefully lift the stencil off and allow the paste/gel to dry. When it's dry, paint the stenciled image with gold paint. Leave it to dry.

→ Punch out some flowers (or other shapes) from your spare metal. Tear two narrow strips of watercolor paper and glue the metal flowers onto these strips. Embellish your punched shapes with beads. (I stitched a bead onto the center of each flower.) Then glue the strips of paper to one of your embossed metal background panels.

→ Weave narrow strips of plain metal through an embossed background panel. Simply cut slits into the background metal. Then cut some narrow strips from your remaining plain metal and weave them through the slits.

→ Place three layers of water-soluble paper onto your deeply etched stamp. Wet the layers and press the paper into the stamp with your fingers. Leave the paper in place overnight to dry. Once dry, remove it from the stamp and glue the shape onto an embossed metal background. Color with acrylic paint.

→ Cut three small squares from your spare embossed metal and punch a small hole in the center of each square. Glue a manufactured silk flower into each hole. Paint the edges of the squares with gold paint and glue the squares to an embossed metal background.

→ Rub a clear embossing stamp pad randomly on an embossed metal background. Sprinkle on ultra-thick embossing powders in a variety of colors and heat with a heat gun. While the embossing powder is still hot, press a rubber stamp into it.

assembly

1 Decide on the number of embossed metal background panels that you want to include on your wall hanging.

2 Arrange them on unbleached cotton backed with felt.

3 Machine stitch each panel to the cotton background, leaving a margin between the panels.

4 Tear strips of patterned cotton fabric and lay them in the margins between the panels; handstitch with fly (at right) and straight stitches to hold the strips in place. ✳

fly stitch

METAL heads
image transfers on metal

by **janette schuster**

Metal Queen (see page 141)

I love attending art workshops, don't you? I always learn new techniques from creative individuals who inspire me to apply what I've learned to my own art. Such was the case a few years ago when I sat in on a collage workshop taught by Claudine Hellmuth. After learning how Claudine transfers photocopied images onto canvas, I was bursting with ideas. As soon as I got home, I started experimenting. Eventually I tried the technique on some metal flashing I had lying around, and I struck gold, so to speak. After much trial and error, I came away with a method for transferring images onto metal.

PREPARE TO TRANSFER
choose the image

Typically, I work with vintage photographs of people (mostly black and white and some color), but any image type that can be photocopied can be used. I find my vintage photo portraits at flea markets, antique stores, and postcard shows. When choosing an image to transfer, I look for one that has sharp, dark details with white highlights and few medium tones. I want an image that, when photocopied, will produce a high-contrast, black-and-white copy with little gray. You get the best results with a photo that has a lot of dark details that will photocopy as black. On a photocopy, the black areas have abundant toner and they transfer well. Gray areas have less toner to transfer, so they come out spotty, if at all. Light or white areas contain little or no toner, so they don't transfer at all. Before copying, you may want to retouch (remove the background or unwanted details), crop, or adjust the darkness of the image using computer software or by hand.

DIRECTIONS

1   Photocopy your image using a black-and-white toner photocopier (not an ink-jet copier, not a color toner copier set on black and white). Adjust the darkness as needed on the copier. I suggest you make multiple copies of the same image, using a range of settings from dark to light, until you find the setting that works best for your image. Also, I find that the copier's text setting works better than the photo setting for this technique.

---

tips

➡ Use a fresh toner copy, made that day if possible. Fresh copies transfer more consistently than old copies.

➡ Try copies from different sources. Copy stores vary in terms of the quality of the toner and paper they use. If you don't get good results with one store's copies, try another.

➡ Start with small images (about 2" [5 cm] square). Once you

materials

- ☐ Image, such as a vintage photograph
- ☐ Aluminum flashing (sold in rolls or small sheets)
- ☐ Kitchen scouring pad
- ☐ Black-and-white toner photocopier
- ☐ Masking tape
- ☐ Iron or woodburning tool with a transfer point
- ☐ Masonite or other ironing surface
- ☐ 2 small spring clamps with plastic tips removed (so they won't melt on your iron)

optional

- ☐ Computer, scanner, and imaging software
- ☐ Pencil
- ☐ Insulated kitchen mitt or pliers with insulated handles
- ☐ Ultra-fine point permanent black marker
- ☐ Goof Off or nail polish remover
- ☐ Rag

I get the best results with images such as these. They have sharp, dark features with some white areas for contrast. By adjusting the darkness on the copier, I get high contrast photocopies that transfer well.

master the technique on a small scale, then progress to larger images.

2. Trim the photocopy, leaving a border around the image. Leave an extra-wide border at the bottom to act as a pulling tab. (If you don't have room for a wide border, create a pulling tab using a white label or tape stuck to the bottom of the copy and then folded back on itself.)

3. Using scissors or metal shears, cut a generous piece of aluminum flashing several times bigger than your image. Allow enough aluminum so that, when your image is transferred in the center of the piece, you will be able to wrap a metal border around the edges of a wood base (see *Metal Heads*, page 140).

4. Using a circular motion, rub the aluminum with a scouring pad. This dulls the shine and gives the metal some tooth.

5. Flip the copy over and hold it up to a light source. On the back of the copy, use a pencil to trace the outline of the image and the position of facial features. (This will help you focus your efforts in the next step.)

- - - - - - - - - - - - - - - - -

tips

→ For ease in cutting and bending the metal, use the thinnest, most flexible aluminum flashing you can find.

→ Try either side of the flashing. Try different brands of flashing. One may work better for you than another.

→ If you can't find aluminum flashing, cut up an aluminum can and use the undecorated side. Try other metals such as copper flashing or craft foil.

heat things up

To transfer a toner copy image to aluminum, I simulate what takes place in a copier. Toner consists of black pigment and meltable plastic. In a copier, heat and pressure melt toner and embed it in fibrous paper. I use the heat of an old iron and pressure (of the iron and my meager muscles) to remelt a copy's toner and adhere it to nonfibrous metal. Remember you are

melting plastic, so work in a well-ventilated area.

Think twice before you use your best clothing iron for this technique. The iron will get scratched and covered with toner. I suggest you dedicate an old iron just for making transfers. Look for used irons at yard sales and flea markets. I often spot them at church rummage sales and thrift stores for a song. I find that vintage electric irons, the heavy chrome variety from the mid-twentieth century, work best. The very reason they became obsolete—they get extremely hot and weigh a ton—is also the reason they produce the best transfers. But if you don't have an old iron, you can get decent results with any iron that gets really hot, as long as the iron's surface isn't damaged; this could scratch your transfer.

1. Work on a smooth, hard surface that can take the heat. I work standing at an ironing board covered with a scrap piece of Masonite. (Find a comfortable position, because your back and arms get a workout with this technique.)

2 Place the copy facedown in the center of the aluminum. To anchor the copy, tape the top and along one side, leaving the pulling tab free. Do not cover the back of the image with tape. Fold back the pulling tab so it will be easier to grasp.

3 Clamp the aluminum to the Masonite.

4 Set your iron on the highest setting and preheat the iron for about five minutes.

5 Begin heating the copy by pressing down on it with the flat body of the iron for a few seconds. This helps tack down the copy.

6 Starting at the bottom of the image near the tab, use the tip or edge of the iron to rub a small section of the back of the copy. Don't rub so hard that you tear the copy paper; rub gently rather than vigorously. Be sure to rub all over the image, concentrating on important details like the facial features that you traced earlier.

7 With the flat of the iron, press the section you rubbed to reheat it, then slowly slide the iron aside as you lift the tab to peel back the paper and peek under it. If that section of the image has transferred sufficiently to the aluminum, leave the paper peeled back and don't reheat that section. When you reheat a transferred section, you run the risk of remelting and transferring the toner back onto the paper. If that section of the image has not

transferred sufficiently, rub and reheat that section until more toner transfers to the metal.

8 Repeat this procedure (rubbing, reheating, and peeling back), working in small sections and moving from the bottom of the image to the top, until the entire image is transferred.

9 Shut off the iron and let the transfer cool before handling it.

tips

➡ Some scorching of the back of the copy is inevitable, but an iron that scorches is likely to burn the toner to the point where it no longer transfers onto the aluminum. To avoid scorching as much as possible, keep the iron moving or turn it down a bit.

➡ Remember to keep peeling back the copy a bit and peeking beneath to see how the transfer is progressing. Peel back the paper while it is still hot, or the toner may be too cool and the paper will stick to the metal and tear.

➡ Some scratching of the aluminum by the iron is inevitable. I suggest you embrace the scratches as happy accidents and even enhance them later to help age the transfer.

In place of an iron, you can try using a woodburning tool with a transfer point. I use this tool only for transferring small images because the tool loses its heat very quickly to the highly conductive aluminum. It also starts out so hot that it scorches the paper. Follow the previous steps, except with these changes:

CAUTIONS

➡ Be very careful using the hot iron. Don't touch any part but the handle. Don't leave the hot iron unattended. Shut off the iron between transfers.

➡ Be careful when peeling back the paper tab. To avoid burning your fingers, consider using an insulated kitchen mitt or pliers with insulated handles.

1 Place a sheet of white scrap paper on the Masonite. After preheating the tool, first cool the tip down a bit by pressing it in a circular motion on the scrap paper until it stops scorching.

2 As you transfer your copy, keep the transfer point moving in a circular motion as you press it flat down on the copy.

3 Transfer the image in small sections. You will need to stop several times and let the tool heat up again to complete the transfer.

4 I recommend letting your transfer set overnight. I find that the contrast between the aluminum and the toner changes subtly and improves after a few hours. Often what I think is just a mediocre transfer looks better to me the next day.

5 Remove any remaining tape and paper from the aluminum. Working in a well-ventilated area, you can remove tape residue and unwanted sections of the transfer with Goof Off or nail polish remover on a rag. I often remove

Lucky

the background of a transferred portrait this way.

6   You can also touch up an imperfect transfer with an ultra-fine point permanent black marker. Use a light hand, adding dots or small dashes and smearing the ink with your finger to soften it where needed.

Once you have a metal transfer, you can cut, hammer, drill, and embellish your way to a cool metal photo collage.

metal heads *collage*

DIRECTIONS

1   Using a handsaw and miter box, cut the wood base to the desired length. I use a furring strip cut to a length of 2¾" (7 cm) for a single transferred image and 7¼" (18.5 cm) for a collage of three transferred images. Sand any rough edges.

2   Decide how you want to position the images on the wood base. Starting with the first transfer, bend and wrap one edge of the aluminum around the edge of the wood to cover it. Trim any excess aluminum with scissors.

3   Using an awl and a hammer, make a starter hole in the wood and the metal before hammering in the nails. Attach the metal to the wood, being careful to hold the nail steady while hammering so that the nail doesn't bend.

4   Continue attaching each edge of the transfer this way, cutting a notch out of the metal at each corner. Attach any additional transfers to the base the same way.

5   Embellish your metal heads with found objects, hats, and other adornments of your choice. Cut hats out of colorful tins and aluminum cans. Smooth any sharp edges with an emery board. Punch or drill holes in your embellishments using an

additional materials

- ☐ Wood for base
- ☐ Handsaw
- ☐ Miter box
- ☐ Sandpaper
- ☐ Hammer
- ☐ 19-gauge × ½" (1.3 cm) steel wire nails or brads
- ☐ Small awl (such as a book awl, needle awl, or dart)
- ☐ Needle- or flat-nose pliers
- ☐ Industrial strength adhesive such as E6000
- ☐ Embellishments such as tins, cans, tape measures, keys, watch parts, brass charms, and game pieces
- ☐ Emery board
- ☐ Metal punch, hand drill, or Dremel with 1/16" (2 mm) or smaller drill bit
- ☐ Ballpoint pen

optional

- ☐ Rubber mallet
- ☐ Sawtooth hanger
- ☐ Colored pencils or markers

awl, metal punch, or drill and nail them in place (remember to pierce a starter hole). Or, attach embellishments with industrial strength glue. You can also embellish your collage with nails and brads.

6   Sign your collage by scratching your signature with a ballpoint pen. If you wish to hang your collage, attach a sawtooth hanger to the back.

tips

➡ Use a rubber mallet to help wrap the metal around the edge of the wood base.

➡ Don't discount the humble cookie tin or aluminum soda can as an embellishment. They often sport great colors and text.

➡ Try hand coloring your metal heads with colored pencils or permanent markers.

➡ If your embellishments become warped by cutting and drilling, flatten them using a rubber mallet.

1   Follow the steps above, this time cutting a base from salvaged wood.

2   Instead of wrapping the aluminum around the base, trim down the transfer, leaving ⅛" to ¼" (3 to

metal Queen collage

additional materials

☐ Salvaged wood

☐ Brass escutcheon pins

6 mm) all around the image. Position the image on the wood and partially attach it using brads (remember to pierce starter holes).

3   Cut clothing out of a colorful cookie tin. Attach the tin just as you would aluminum, but use brass escutcheon pins. Embellish with found objects such as a wood ruler, a metal tape measure, and decorative found metals. Attach the embellishments as described earlier.

4   Sign your collage on the front or back. If you wish, attach a sawtooth hanger to the back. ✳

DIPPED AND *delightful*
PAPER BEADS

by **kelli nina perkins**

From the time we pick up our first crayon to the time we stand and admire our adult handiwork, we are taking the elemental experience of making art with our hands and branding it with our unique presence. There is a comforting simplicity in those crafts we learned as children that makes them an ideal launching point for true artistic adventure. Making paper beads can be as simple as rolling construction paper with paste and painting it with nail polish or as satisfyingly complex as multilayered wonders that emulate the fanciest lampwork beads.

As early as the end of the nineteenth century, Victorian divas gathered around the dining room table to roll great mounds of beads to string as fancy room dividers. Ladies' magazines touted the beauty of paper jewels made from wallpaper, one of the most plentiful scrap materials available in the infancy of machine-made paper. In those simpler times, women made use of what was on hand, including that new wonder, the department store catalog. Sunday comics, magazines, and junk mail have all found their way into handmade beads. Vintage bead collectors recount carefully unrolling their delicate paper treasures to find turn-of-the-century advertisements inside. The least likely material often produces the most interesting result.

Today, paper is perhaps the most basic art supply. It's available everywhere and many of us continue our love affair with it throughout our lives. Now nearly everyone has access to a wide range of handmade or imported papers that are glorious art in themselves.

Your favorite paper, in bead form, can embellish everything from quilts to earrings. Don't discount those small scraps left over from other projects—they're welcome here and might be just the thing to add a splash of color or visual interest.

Because paper beads are so simple to make, you can whip up a dozen in less than an hour. By making your own, you won't have to struggle to find the right color bead for your current project. So get ready to raid your art stash and ban the common bead.

CUTTING

1   Select papers for your beads. Each piece should be at least 6" to 8" (15 to 20.5 cm) long. If you are making a whole batch of paper beads for later use, lay out a variety of papers in different colors, thicknesses, and visual variety. Be sure to include recycled items, which often yield the most interesting results. These include magazine pages, book text, maps, sheet music, newspaper, comics, and accidental papers created during other projects.

materials

- [ ] Assorted recycled, commercial, or hand-decorated papers
- [ ] Scissors or paper cutter
- [ ] Freezer paper or other nonstick surface
- [ ] Matte gel medium
- [ ] Brush
- [ ] Plastic straws
- [ ] Waxed paper
- [ ] Small dowel rods (whittled to a point) or wooden skewers
- [ ] Masking tape
- [ ] Boss Gloss Embossing Ink
- [ ] Ultra Thick Embossing Enamel (clear)
- [ ] Heat gun
- [ ] Heat-proof dish
- [ ] Aluminum foil

optional

- [ ] **Wraps:** wire, metallic threads, thin fibers, Angelina fibers
- [ ] **Dips:** embossing, distressing, or Pearl Ex powders, art glitter, seed beads or micro-beads, Angelina fibers, wire, metallic thread, tinsel, Beadazzles, mica dust, gold flakes

You'll also want to have some tiny scraps of color on hand to add interest after the bead is rolled.

2   Cut strips for your bead base. A rectangle (1½" × 7" [3.8 × 18 cm]) or a triangle (1½" [3.8 cm] at the base and tapering to a point about 7" [18 cm] long) are good basic shapes. Cut as many as you think you'll want for your bead session. Vary the shape of the base to achieve other interesting looks. The length of each strip depends on the thickness of the paper, so use 6" to 8" (15 to 20.5 cm) as a starting point, cutting longer strips for thinner paper and shorter strips for thick papers. The width of the base will be the overall length of your bead and can range from ½" to 2" (1.3 to 5 cm).

- - - - - - - - - - - - - - - - - - -
tip: Tissue papers are more suitable for layering atop other papers. Otherwise, you must use a very long strip to get a bead that is thick enough to hold up to use. Handmade papers only need to go around the straw a few times, so cut them shorter. Don't forget that you can layer, so, if your original bead base is too small, wrap some more paper around it to achieve the look you want.

- - - - - - - - - - - - - - - - - - -
tip: If you'd like, you can make templates out of cardstock, then draw and cut your triangles. I prefer to use the wild approach and just start cutting slivers of triangles, alternating with rectangles, and just mixing them up. A paper cutter is faster, but scissors will do.

In addition to the base papers, cut some smaller bits—tiny triangles ¼" (6 mm) wide and about 2" (5 cm) long, or narrow strips you can wrap around your bead bases.

ROLLING

Many paper-bead methods require that you string the beads until dry. With this method you won't have to.

1   Lay a base strip, decorative side down, on a nonstick work surface (such as freezer paper) with the wide end toward you. Brush the paper with a thin coat of gel medium, starting about ½" (1.3 cm) in from the end closest to you. Gel medium works best because it dries fast and holds well. I have found that using a glue stick will

leave beads popping open before you get to the next step.

2   Lay a plastic drinking straw along the unglued edge of the strip and start rolling the paper up along the straw. Choose a straw that is the approximate size you want the inside of your bead to be and keep the rolling tight for a stronger bead. Wipe down the straw with a little olive oil every few beads to counteract the gel medium and keep the beads sliding easily.

tip: When rolling rectangles, go for uniformity and straight lines at the edges. When rolling triangles, try to end up with the final point right in the center of the bead. If your edges are off or your bead is too long (mine often is!) don't worry. After the bead is dry you can snip the edges with a pair of scissors.

3   Glue on some smaller strips in a contrasting color. My favorite trick is to add some words or text from a discarded book. You can't go wrong, so just pick some fun scraps and glue them on with gel medium.

4   Use rubber-stamped or printed images, text, or even cancelled stamps to decorate the outer layer of your bead. You can also draw on them with markers, paint them, roll them on iridescent inkpads or use oil pastels to decorate them.

5   Slide your completed bead off the end of the straw and onto a piece of waxed paper to dry while you make more. Vary the widths and shapes of the beads you make for more interest.

After you've made a mound of beads, the real fun begins. This is where you'll leave elementary school in the dust! With such interesting materials available, the mundane bead is no more. You can wrap some of your beads or go directly to dipping.

WRAPPING

The beads are ready for the next step when they are no longer tacky—that should only take a few minutes.

1   Dab the bead with a glue stick and wind your wrap around a few times. Try wrapping some of them in whatever you have on hand: wire in various colors, metallic threads, or thin fibers.

2   Once wrapped, press the end of the wrapping material into the gel medium. You only need to make sure the wrap adheres until they're dipped.

tip: Thick wraps like fibers can make your bead bulky; be careful to choose fibers that fit the project at hand.

DIPPING

Assemble a dipping station as if you were going to be making ice cream sundaes. Cover a heatproof dish with aluminum foil to act as a catchall for flying embossing powder and to avoid burning your countertops. For the toppings, include various colors of embossing, distressing, and Pearl Ex powders, seed beads and microbeads, Beadazzles, etc.—whatever catches your fancy. Remember that some beads may be worn next to the skin as jewelry, so avoid anything too sharp or so large that it might make your bead lumpy and therefore uncomfortable.

tip: With some materials, you can dip right into the jars, but for others such as seed beads, gold flakes, or Angelina, lay a small amount out on a sheet of freezer paper so that you can roll the hot beads in them.

directions

1   Wrap your dowel (or skewer) with masking tape, using enough tape to keep the bead securely in place when it is slid on. Pop a bead on the end of the dowel rod. The end of the stick should not be visible on the other side of the bead.

2   Tap the bead with Boss Gloss all the way around and then dip it in clear Ultra Thick Embossing Enamel (UTEE). Use a heat gun to melt the clear coating and, while it's still warm, re-dip in UTEE and reheat.

CAUTION: Working with a heat gun requires some caution. Make sure it's plugged into a GFCI (ground fault circuit interrupter) outlet and never let it make contact with countertops or your skin.

3   Working quickly, dip the hot bead into another material like Pearl Ex or glitter, then apply the heat gun again to melt the new material into the clear UTEE, then dip it back into the UTEE and remelt.

Sunflower Fantasy 12" × 12" (30.5 × 30.5 cm)

4 Continue this process of dipping into UTEE, heating, dipping into your "sundae toppings," and then back into the UTEE. Don't let the coating get too hot and keep turning the bead to avoid drips.

- - - - - - - - - - - - - - - -

tip: Think of the bead as two halves; you will be working on one end and then turning the bead over on the dowel to work on the other end. At any point you can roll the bead across the toppings you have sprinkled on waxed paper to incorporate them into a layer, as well.

5 Finish the open edge of the bead by dipping it in metallic UTEE or regular embossing powder and heating and melting it again. Now lay your stick across the heatproof dish so that the bead is suspended while you work on the next bead. When the first bead has cooled, pop it off the stick and turn it over to finish the other half. You can vary the colors so that each side is different if you like.

6 When the bead is done, run a skewer through it to loosen any leftover toppings and make sure the hole is free for stringing.

- - - - - - - - - - - - - - - -

Variation: Prop the heat gun on a stable, heatproof surface and heat the bead. Then, with your free hand, gently sprinkle a little metallic embossing powder on your hot bead. It will melt instantly and make a lovely speckled effect.

- - - - - - - - - - - - - - - -

tip: Be sure not to plug the hole of your bead as you dip. If you accidentally do this, gently apply heat to the end of the bead until it's soft enough to run a stick through it and clear out the excess. ✳

CHAPTER **7**

get your ART OUT THERE!

After you've completed your art, what's your plan? If you don't want to be the only collector of your treasures, you need to be sure the world sees them and gets to know you. In this chapter, you'll find the scoop on online art and craft marketplaces such as Etsy and some new ideas for getting your art to the front lines.

heavens to ETSY!

by **cate coulacos prato**

Handmade sketchbooks by Lucie Summers, an Etsy seller.

Until fairly recently, selling your artwork has been a cumbersome, time-consuming process. Galleries and boutiques are hard to get into, and many take a hefty percentage of your profit. Craft shows are fun, but exhausting, and you only reach a small segment of the population. It can be difficult to attract the right customers (i.e., lovers of handmade art) to your personal websites or eBay auctions amid the sea of merchandise, and the fee structure makes selling inexpensive items not worthwhile.

Enter Etsy.com, the self-proclaimed marketplace for buying and selling all things handmade.

Launched in June 2005, the Brooklyn-based company was founded by a group of twenty-somethings inspired to promote handmade (instead of mass-produced) items all over the world and reconnect makers with buyers. Today, Etsy is a virtual worldwide community of mixed-media artists, knitters, painters, quilters, glassblowers, furniture makers—you name it. Etsy sellers number in the hundreds of thousands. Some artists have made a full-time career out of Etsy, selling one-of-a-kind belts, paintings, and underwear, plus crafting supplies and raw materials, including vintage papers and found objects.

"It's proven to be a valuable marketing tool alone. And, without a doubt, it has significantly helped to support me financially," says mixed-media artist Kelly Rae Roberts. "Instead of having to do a ton of footwork to get my work in boutiques, galleries, where I'd perhaps get a small commission, Etsy allows me to take home great profit with relative ease. I know several people who have been able to support themselves, mortgages and all, on Etsy sales alone."

Mixed-media artist Christina Romeo started using Etsy out of curiosity, but says, "I quickly attained a little following of mixed-media textile lovers and was selling enough to give me some extra cash on the side."

It's fairly easy to set up shop on Etsy. You simply need some handmade items, a computer hooked up to the Internet, a digital camera to take images of your handmade items, and a credit card, which Etsy holds on file. Some sellers, particularly those who have more sophisticated computer skills, can find Etsy lacks some technical finesse: there were some bugs and glitches, especially when it first launched. But overall, artists say Etsy is fast and easy to use.

"I'm quite a technophobe, and Etsy is really, really easy to set up a shop front on," says artist Lucie Summers. "And if there's something you don't know, there's a brilliant forums section where you can ask questions. I've learned a lot about resolution and dpi!"

Many artists say one of the things they like about Etsy is its reasonable fee structure (for every item you place in your Etsy storefront, Etsy charges a small fee and takes a commission on the sale of your item).

Buying on Etsy requires setting up an account, which takes minutes. Shopping could take hours, though, given not only the thousands of items for sale, but also the myriad ways Etsy organizes them: by category, color, geographic location, previous purchases, other people's favorites, gift occasions, and what other people just bought, to name a few. The choices can be overwhelming, and some tools are more effective than others. For example, shopping by color is fun, but clicking on periwinkle will get you periwinkle felted beads—and also orange earrings on a purplish-blue backdrop.

Prices on Etsy range from a couple of dollars on up. To establish your prices, it helps to research what other artists charge for similar work online. And don't forget to factor in materials, time, and the Etsy commission.

"Market research is the key. You need to price items as if they are in brick-and-mortar shops, because if you are asked to supply wholesale, you need to be able to make some money and not do it for pennies. I make more on some stuff than I do on others, but that's the way of the world," Lucie says.

Successful Etsy sellers say you can drive traffic to your site by sending out a shop announcement via email or on your blog; tagging other artists' sites as favorites (which often prompts them to tag you in return); raising your profile in the forums by helping other users; and listing products often—even daily—to keep people coming back.

Beyond buying and selling, however, artists love the community-building aspect of Etsy.

"I definitely think it has a few kinks to work out for sellers, but all in all, it's been wonderful," Kelly says. "The timing of Etsy could not have been better. The crafty movement really needed a site like this one to support it. People are really passionate about supporting Etsy, and it's been fantastic to be part of it." ✳

Mixed-media quilt by Christina Romeo, an Etsy seller.

10 TIPS for SELLING YOUR ART
during hard times

Breathe 5" × 5" (12.5 × 12.5 cm) Print by Kelly Rae Roberts.

It wasn't that long ago that artists were basking in the green glow of cash from society's love affair with purchasing handmade objects and the burgeoning technology with which to sell them. Etsy boutiques would empty quicker than you could say "Paypal." Online art auctions yielded enough profit for creators and their favorite charities. Gallery sales boomed.

Lately, not so much.

We asked some artists on the front lines of the selling wars—some veterans and some recent recruits—how they're making it through these tough economic times. All the artists we interviewed said that while sales may be down, their spirits aren't. While being realistic, they were surprisingly upbeat. In fact, being upbeat is part of their strategy.

GEOFFREY GORMAN

When we reached Geoffrey Gorman, he was in the midst of preparing a talk on marketing strategies for artists. The mixed-media sculptor worked in galleries for ten years and has also assisted artists with the business side of art. He has a three-pronged strategy for weathering the down economy. The first is altering his artwork somewhat.

"I am creating smaller pieces, and, on the advice of my gallery dealer, making my pieces more cheerful and positive. I'm also reworking and recycling older pieces to make them more accessible to my buyers," he says. Geoffrey is also relying on his skills as a teacher and business mentor, leading more marketing workshops and consulting one-to-one with artists.

He's also using his blog and website to keep in contact with clients and his network. "This is a time where our relationships are critical, whether they are with our clients, or our agents and gallery dealers. The people who are making sales are working harder than ever. I'm seeing that gallery dealers are selling to their longtime clients and friends," he says.

KELLY RAE ROBERTS

Painter and collage artist Kelly Rae Roberts says that after three years of briskly selling her artwork online, she had to offer her first sale during the winter holidays.

"It was a great success, but it would have been a financially slow month had I not offered $10 off my prints for the month of December," she says.

She has stepped up her marketing tactics, blogging and sending out e-newsletters more frequently, and plans to continue keeping her prices low. But she's not changing her art.

"I notice that when I start trying too hard to make items I think will sell, I don't enjoy the process as much. So it's important that I keep doing and making what I love and hope for the best," says Kelly Rae. This positive outlook serves her well in another way, she says. "I think people, on a collective front, want positive messages of hope in this economy. So offering affordable artwork with messages of a hopeful spirit can be a great way to stay afloat. I've noticed my small, affordable affirmation prints are selling really well at the moment."

CLAUDINE HELLMUTH

Collage artist, teacher, and author Claudine Hellmuth, who recently introduced her own line of art supplies, says her custom artwork sold at full speed through the holiday season, when people were buying gifts. However, later in the winter she experienced a slowdown, and she predicts that people will continue to be careful about how they spend their money.

"They might not spend the money to take a full-day class, but they will decide that they can sign up for online classes instead," Claudine says, noting that her online workshops have been filling up quickly. "For artworks, I see people wanting to buy the smaller-ticket items, so they can still purchase art, but with less expense."

Claudine's custom artwork is time-consuming to make, so lowering prices on it is not an option. However, she's working on some new, less expensive items she can sell to buyers who like her work but can't afford the custom art. She's also trying to promote herself more.

"In the past I might have let some things slide a little, like updating my website, adding new items, or doing promotion. Now, I am committing myself to these tasks with renewed energy and using the Internet to my advantage to discover new clients.

"I am sure there are many artists out there who will only feel a slight pinch in this economy. Remember, if people really want your work, they will find a way to purchase it! They might have to save longer, but they will find a way," Claudine says.

top tips

→ **Promote yourself.** Start a blog. Get on Facebook. Twitter away. If you already have a blog, blog more often. You want to remind people that you're still there, still creating great art.

→ **Avoid lowering your prices overall.** If you're an established artist, you have most likely arrived at a fair price for your everyday work, and lowering the price would not only devalue it now, but also make it harder to bring prices back up when the economy improves. However, the occasional "discount day" or holiday sale can help stimulate purchases. (Be sure to publicize any special offers through e-media and other networks.) Consider offering payment plans to special customers or on big-ticket items.

→ **Offer a variety of price points.** To make your artwork more affordable to larger numbers of people, try making some items that can carry a lower price tag, such as prints of paintings, greeting cards, smaller artwork pieces, and gift items such as jewelry.

→ **Make your art useful.** Customers who may not be able to justify spending money on a wall hanging might be persuaded to buy a funky clutch, fabric bowl, or book wrap.

→ **Cut back on business expenses.** If you're attending a show or craft fair, can you stay with a friend instead of in a hotel or share a room with another artist or two? Do you really need those fancy little business cards, or can you get creative with rubber stamps and cardstock? How about pairing up with another artist and sending e-newsletters together, splitting the cost?

→ **Consider shipping costs.** If possible, create art that is less expensive to ship. Avoid heavy pieces in awkward sizes.

→ **Keep up your professional relationships.** Stay in touch with gallery owners, clients, and other professional contacts. Just because a gallery isn't taking art right now doesn't mean that they aren't keeping a file of promising prospects for the future.

→ **Recycle your projects.** Look at past projects and unfinished objects. Can you recycle them into something new? If so, you can save money on materials and make something marketable at the same time.

→ **Offer downloads and freebies.** Free or low-cost downloads (such as patterns or computer wallpaper) keep customers in contact with your work for very little money. You might also consider throwing in a little extra something—an artist trading card, a clutch of fabric or found objects—in outgoing packages to add value and bring customers back for more.

→ **Send a positive message.** You have to be true to yourself and your art, but keep in mind that very dark and depressing art may not sell well right now.

WENDY RICHARDSON

"People are looking more and spending less," says fiber artist Wendy Richardson. "Customers say to me, 'if I'm going to spend money, it's got to be something I really want.'"

As a result, Wendy has added some new products to her wares, pricing them at about $20. She's also repackaged her bundles of overdyed fabrics, offering fewer pieces at a lower cost, to give customers a more affordable choice.

"Customers are happy if they can buy something from you without spending a fortune. It also seems to help if it is something they can actually use," she says.

Wendy has also cut back on her own expenses, from the cost of doing business to fewer dinners out, and she recently took a teaching job to bring in some extra income.

She offers this advice: "Be flexible, simplify, be creative. Don't panic—I try never to let my customers know I'm stressed about the economy. Use any extra time you have to your advantage, creating new work and new products. And don't forget to network."

LESLEY RILEY

Artist Lesley Riley is also using the Internet to her advantage, using giveaways on her blog to increase traffic and attract people to her books and other merchandise.

"Even if someone does not win a giveaway, they may be more likely to make a purchase because of all the excitement and interest a giveaway brings," says Lesley.

The way to thrive as an artist in this economic climate, she advises, is to follow the three Ps: pricing, promotion, and personality.

"Price your art right, promote it and yourself, and let people know the person behind the art. If you can make a personal connection with potential buyers, you're more than halfway to a sale," she says, adding, "I would suggest that this is not the time to retreat. People are attracted to success and confidence. If you believe in the value of your art, others will believe in it, too. And that also means do not reduce your prices. It's okay to have specials or a discount day, but across-the-board price reductions reflect poorly on how you value yourself and your art," Lesley says.

"Use this slow time to produce, produce, produce," she adds. "New ideas and inspiration will come from the work, and you'll be ready when times are good again." ✳

Susan Andrews and Carolyn Fellman have shared studios, travels, and projects for more than twenty years. Known as The Oiseaux Sisters, they migrate seasonally from New York to Florida and teach at both ends of the road. They spend part of each year traveling and conducting workshops all over the world.
oiseauxsisters.com

Laura Cater-Woods is a working studio artist with an extensive exhibition record and numerous awards. A compulsive mark maker, Laura lives in Montana where she gardens, takes morning walks along the Yellowstone River, and tries to find the perfect balance between studio time and everything else.
cater-woods.com

June Pfaff Daley is a mixed-media artist who creates with everything from wood to fabric. She enjoys transforming thrift-store treasures and favors whimsical motifs. June resides in Cincinnati, Ohio, with three fantastic kids, her supportive husband, and two charming cats.
junepfaffdaley.com

Dorit Elisha is a mixed-media artist, instructor, and the author of *Printmaking + Mixed Media* (Interweave, 2009). Her favorite media are printmaking, bookmaking, fiber art, and collage. Recycled and found objects are her favorite sources for art materials. Dorit's artwork has been displayed in galleries around the United States and published in magazines and books.
doritelisha.com

Patricia Gaignat is a mixed-media artist living in Long Island, New York. She enjoys printmaking, bookmaking, journaling, sewing, painting, sketching, and making her own stamps. Patricia works with paper, fabric, encaustic wax, and even a bit of metal and wood.
reclinerart.posterous.com.

Lisa Kesler is a nationally recognized painter and printmaker who finds inspiration through experimentation. The images in her work are often stylized or abstracted forms inspired by the rural Illinois countryside where she resides. Lisa's contemporary artwork can be found in private and corporate collections throughout the United States.
lisakesler.com

Jane LaFazio truly believes she is living the life she was meant to live. She has cultivated a wide range of skills as a painter, mixed-media and quilt artist, and art teacher. She is well known for her fun-loving teaching style. Jane's artwork is featured in Danny Gregory's book *An Illustrated Life* (How, 2008).
plainjanestudio.com

Susie Lafond has a passion for mixed-media art and art journals and continues to challenge the boundaries of what a journal can be. She is a contributing artist for several books, magazines, and zines. Susie sells her one-of-a-kind, multi-spine journals on Etsy.com.
mylifeonebitatatime.blogspot.com

Jenn Mason enjoys encouraging others to live more creatively every day. She is a wife, mother, artist, sister, daughter, author, singer-in-the-shower, period movie fan, lover of laughter, designer, teacher, friend, and editor of *Cloth Paper Scissors* magazine.
jennmason.com

Annette Morgan is an award-winning quilter, author, teacher, and qualified quilt judge and tutor. She teaches City & Guilds courses in England to diploma level, and she enjoys experimenting with unusual techniques, trying to keep one step ahead of her students! All things textile are her passion.
annettemorgan.co.uk

Elizabeth St. Hilaire Nelson uses torn bits of handpainted papers to make her unique and vibrant collages. A first-place winner in the collage category for *The Artist's Magazine* in 2010, this multitalented artist plays violin with the Maitland Symphony Orchestra in Florida and is a professional graphic designer.
nelsoncreative.com

Jacqueline Newbold is a watercolor artist who loves to explore creative ways to incorporate mixed media into her art. Using a warm and playful color palette, she captures moments in time in her travel journals. Jacqueline loves to combine travel and art and conducts group painting trips near her home in Bend, Oregon, and abroad.
djnewbold.blogspot.com

Lisa Occhipinti is a mixed-media painter, book artist, and author of *The Repurposed Library* (Stewart Tabori & Chang, 2011), a book of thirty-three book-art projects. Her work is in private and corporate collections worldwide. Lisa lives and works in Venice, California, where she teaches privately.
locchipinti.com

Jodi Ohl is a mixed-media artist known for her delightfully whimsical paintings. She hosts online classes, conducts workshops, and enjoys writing for a variety of national art magazines, including *Cloth Paper Scissors*. Jodi lives in North Carolina with her two sons, Josh and Zachary.
sweetrepeats.blogspot.com

Sue Pelletier, artist and art teacher, is drawn to objects with a history. Her work is whimsical, quirky, and humorous. Sue's work has been published in *Cloth Paper Scissors* magazine and is featured in the *Cloth Paper Scissors Workshop* DVD *Texture: Build It Up!*. Sue lives in Hopkinton, Massachusetts, with her two teenagers and her dogs.
www.suepelletierlaughpaint.com

Kelli Nina Perkins is a mixed-media artist and librarian living on the shores of Lake Michigan. For more than a decade, Kelli has been making art that prizes the everyday ephemera of our lives, incorporating the common flotsam of discarded life in her art. She is the author of *Stitch Alchemy: Combining Fabric + Paper for Mixed Media Art* (Interweave, 2009).
ephemeralalchemy.blogspot.com

DJ Pettitt enjoys painting with acrylics on many different substrates, creating journals and art books, doing photography, and teaching art workshops nationally, internationally, and online. Creating is essential to her and a large part of who she is.
djpettitt.com

Cate Coulacos Prato is a writer and editor, most recently for *Cloth Paper Scissors Studios* magazine. Currently, she is the editor of quiltingarts.com. She is also the author of *Inside the Creative Studios: Inspiration and Ideas for Your Art and Craft Space* (Interweave, 2011) and *Mixed-Media Self-Portraits: Inspiration and Techniques* (Interweave, 2008). She lives with her family and many pets in central Massachusetts.

Patricia Baldwin Seggebruch is an avid painter, instructor, and writer who constantly seeks creative outlets and new opportunities. She keeps busy by teaching worldwide, writing, and raising four sons. Patricia is the author of *Encaustic Workshop* (North Light, 2009) and *Encaustic Mixed Media* (North Light, 2011).
gingerfetish.blogspot.com

Viv Sliwka is a passionate collector of vintage textiles, haberdashery, and paper ephemera. Nothing gives her greater pleasure than incorporating a little of the past into her mixed-media art, needle cases, purses, brooches, and textile collages. Viv creates her artwork in her garden studio in Staffordshire, England.
hensteethart.blogspot.com

Janette Schuster is a freelance writer, artist, workshop instructor, and incurable treasure hunter. She indulges her love of found relics by using them in jewelry, collage, and assemblage. Janette's work has appeared in many publications, and she is the author of *Mixed-Media Collage Jewelry: New Directions in Memory Jewelry* (Lark, 2009).
visualapothecary.com

Dawn DeVries Sokol is the author of *1000 Artist Journal Pages* (Quarry, 2008), *Doodle Diary: Art Journaling for Girls* (Gibbs Smith, 2010), and *Doodle Sketchbook: Art Journaling for Boys* (Gibbs Smith, 2011). She is also a book designer and an avid journaler and doodler. Dawn lives in Tempe, Arizona, with her husband, T.J., and her dog, Lucy.
dblogala.com

Jacqueline Sullivan has been studying mixed-media arts and calligraphy for many years. She is a nationally recognized artist and teacher, and has an instructional DVD, *Acrylics: Textures, Layers and Metallics* (Creative Catalyst). Jacqueline has recently begun applying her knowledge of watercolor and acrylic painting to canvas and paper as backgrounds for calligraphic collages.
jacquelinesullivan.com

Beryl Taylor grew up in England and moved to the United States with her family in 2002. She qualified in the City & Guilds Creative Embroidery program and is the author of *Mixed Media Explorations* (Interweave, 2006). Beryl has appeared on *Quilting Arts TV* and has two *Quilting Arts Workshop* DVDs, *Layer by Layer* and *Mixed-Media Art Quilts*.
beryltaylor.com

Lynn Whipple is a Florida native and a lifelong artist. Her work includes collage, writing, drawing, stitching, altered objects, oil painting, songwriting, and guitar. Lynn likes to infuse her work with simplicity, inventiveness, and humor. Her work is shown nationally and has been featured in books and magazines.
lynnwhipple.com

RESOURCES

The following resources offer a wide range of supplies for mixed-media art making.

Cedar Canyon Textiles
cedarcanyontextiles.com
(877) 296-9278
Shiva Artists Paintstiks, tools, and accessories.

Daniel Smith
danielsmith.com
(800) 426-6740
A full selection of art supplies.

Dharma Trading Co.
dharmatrading.com
(800) 542-5227
Textile craft supplies and dyeables.

Faber-Castell USA
faber-castell.us
(216) 643-4660
Colored pencils and other art and graphic supplies.

Golden Artist Colors
goldenpaints.com
(607) 847-6154
Golden acrylic paints, mediums, gessos, grounds, and additives.

I Love to Create
ilovetocreate.com
(800) 438-6226
Aleene's Tacky glue and other glue and collage products.

Interweave Store
Interweavestore.com
Books, DVDs, art quilting and mixed-media art supplies.

Rubert, Gibbon & Spyder
jacquardproducts.com
(800) 442-0455
Jacquard textile paints, dyes, and textile art supplies.

Liquitex
liquitex.com
(888) 422-7954
Liquitex acrylic paints, mediums, gessos, grounds, and additives.

Polyform Products Company
sculpey.com
Sculpey polymer clay.

R&F Products
rfpaints.com
(800) 206-8088
Encaustic paints, pigments, and supplies.

Ranger Industries
rangerink.com
(732) 389-3535
Ranger inks, Claudine Hellmuth studio products, and other mixed-media art supplies.

Sakura of America
sakuraofamerica.com
Pigment pens, markers, and art supplies.

Walnut Hollow
(800) 395-5995
walnuthollow.com
Wood substrates and woodcarving kits.

→ INDEX

absorbent ground 34
acrylic paint, fluid 20
adhesives 131; fabric 131; gemstone 131; jewelry 131; paper 131; repositioning 21
alcohol 33
Angelina fibers 20
artist trading card (ATC) 20

background techniques 50
backstitch 123
beads, paper 142–147
bone folder 20
bookbinding 67
brayer 20
brushes 20, 21

chain stitch 123
charcoal 32
collage 20, 34–35, 85–89, 100–105, 111–123, 126–130, 140–141
collage, papers for 99
collography 20
color catcher sheets 51
colors 30–31

doodling 71–73
dry brush 20
dryer sheets 51

embellishments 38, 39, 50
encaustic 20, 126–130
Etsy 149–151

fabric paper 20
fabric, commercial 37; water-soluble 21
felt 20
fiber, Angelina 20
finishing embellishments 39
fixative 20
fluid acrylic paint 20
fly stitch 135
focal point 20
Forster, Cornelia (Corni) 19
found objects 37, 85–89, 99

free- motion stitching 20
French knot 123
fusible web 20

gelatin monprints 52–55
gel medium 20
gel pens 20
gesso 20
getting started 10–13
glazes, 109
glue, all-purpose 131; craft and tacky 131; permanent 131; Sobo 21
glossary 20
Gorman, Geoffrey 153

hake brush 21
handstitches 123
heat gun 21
heat-set 21
Hellmuth, Claudine 153

ink, walnut 21
inspiration 17–19

journaling 11, 18–19, 22–25, 79–81

layering 50
letterform 109
Lutradur 51

maps 74–77
matte medium 21
metal 132–141
metallics 32–33
Mod Podge 21
molding paste 21
mulberry paper 21

needle felting 21

paint 29–30
pamphlet stitch 67
paper, alternatives 51; fabric 20; mulberry 21; watercolor 30

paste, molding 21
pens, gel 20
photo transfer 21, 137–140
plastic wrap 34

repositionable adhesive 21
Richardson, Wendy 155
Riley, Lesley 155
Rit dye 34
Roberts, Kelly Rae 153

salt 32
sand 32
satin stitch 123
screen printing 21
selling artwork 149–155
sketching ideas 22–25, 58–61
Sobo glue 21
stabilizer, water-soluble 21
stamps 38
stencils 38
stitching sketches 25
stitching 111–123, free-motion 20; hand- 39; machine 38–39
stippling 21
supplies 14–15

text for collage 107–108
transfers 21, 45–47, 50
Tyvek 51

underpainting 21

walnut ink 21
washes 109
water colors 29
water-soluble fabric 21
water-soluble stabilizer 21
workspace 17

Enjoy more CREATIVE MIXED-MEDIA
ideas AND solutions WITH
THESE INNOVATIVE resources

from Interweave

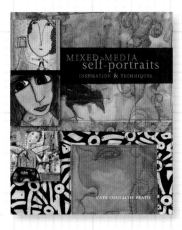

Mixed-Media Self-Portraits
Inspiration & Techniques
Cate Coulacos Prato
ISBN 978-1-59668-082-1
$22.95

Mixed-Media Explorations
*Blending Paper, Fabric, and
Embellishment to Create
Inspired Designs*
Beryl Taylor
ISBN 978-0-97669-282-9
$27.99

Mixed Mania
*Recipes for Delicious
Mixed-Media Creations*
Debbi Crane and Cheryl Prater
ISBN 978-1-59668-084-5
$22.95

cloth·paper·scissors®

Explore the magazine for both beginner and
seasoned artists interested in trying new techniques
and sharing their work and expertise with a greater
audience. Subscribe at Clothpaperscissors.com

ClothPaperScissors.com is the online community
where mixed-media artists come to play and share
creative ideas. Receive expert tips and techniques,
e-newsletters, blogs, forums, videos, special offers,
and more! Join today at Clothpaperscissors.com

shop.clothpaperscissors.com